THE RACE

By
Eliyahu M. Goldratt
and
Robert E. Fox

N

North River Press, Inc.

Copyright © 1986 Creative Output Inc.

Manufactured in the United States of America

Library of Congress Cataloging-in-Publication Data

Goldratt, Eliyahu M., 1948-
The race.

   1.Inventory control. 2. Quality of products.
3. Corporate profits. 4. Efficiency, Industrial.
5. Competition, International. I. Fox, Robert E.,
1937-   . II. Title.
HD40.G65   1986   658.7'87   86-18197
ISBN 0-88427-062-9

For more information on the concepts presented in this book please contact:

Creative Output
Commerce Park
Milford, CT 06460
Tel: (203) 877-5671

For additional copies please contact your local bookstore, Creative Output, or the publisher:

North River Press
Box 241
Croton-on-Hudson, NY 10520
Tel: (914) 941-7175

INTRODUCTION

THE RACE is about our standard of living and how we can increase it. Today, we are facing a real threat in the Western World that the opposite will happen. The threat is not just to us. If our living standard declines, everyone else on this globe is adversely affected.

Both the source and the solution to the problem lie in the same place—manufacturing. Manufacturing has been the major wealth generator of our industrialized world. This ability to generate wealth has made our standard of living the envy of the rest of the world. If we continue to lose our manufacturing base, and we are losing it rapidly, we and everyone else will certainly live less well.

This companion book to Eli Goldratt's and Jeff Cox's underground best seller, THE GOAL, can help you to reverse this situation. Readers of THE GOAL, and they range from the boardroom to the universities to the factory floor to spouses at all levels, report startling improvements just because their company read a business book disguised as a novel, or as some say, a love story.

THE RACE is also an unusual book. Its messages can be grasped simply by looking through the graphics. It can be understood better by reading the accompanying text. It is even more deeply grasped and useful when manufacturing people at all levels discuss its implications and application to their own environment.

The introduction of THE GOAL caused a development we did not expect—GOAL Circles. Action groups of both managers and shop floor employees working to find their "Herbies," cut batch sizes, abandon efficiencies and link marketing actions more closely to manufacturing capabilities. Distribution of some galley proofs of THE RACE seems to be causing the same phenomenon—RACE Circles. Maybe the Western World is developing its own response to the Japanese Quality Circles.

GOAL Circles and RACE Circles are an excellent beginning. Through them companies can begin a process of ongoing improvement. However, one-time improvements, no matter how significant, will not allow us to catch up or stay ahead for long in the increasingly intense race for a competitive edge in which our industries are embroiled. We need to permanently establish and continually improve on a process of ongoing improvement.

THE RACE enables you to derive a superior system—Drum-Buffer-Rope—for generating continual logistical improvements. It also illustrates how to focus on the process improvements that will have the greatest impact on your competitive edge. The epilogue and appendix quizzes will give the thoughtful reader insight in how to initiate and then extend a process of ongoing improvement into other areas like marketing and financial control.

Each step in implementing an increasingly effective process of ongoing improvement will require better understanding and more effective tools. A company often needs to look outside for the insights and products to establish such an approach. We believe, however, that the revolution required in how you run your companies can only be *led* from the inside. The steps required to adopt and manage a process of ongoing improvement are a management responsibility.

The reversal of the fortunes of our manufacturing companies is certainly important to its employees and investors. It may be even more important to each of us and our countries. We wish you much success and hope THE GOAL and THE RACE help to move you in the correct direction.

Eli Goldratt
Bob Fox

1: ARE WE LOSING OUR DOMINANT POSITION?

The Industrial Revolution began in England and spread across Europe and America in the ensuing years. Since that beginning, Western countries have held a predominant position in almost all types of manufacturing. The strength of these industries made our standard of living the envy of the world.

In the last 15 years a dramatic change has occurred. In 1970, it became apparent that we had lost our predominant position in smokestack industries like steel, brass and textiles. Our world market share slipped and plants were closed due to competition from the East. We thought our demise was due to the low-cost labor and modern equipment of our competitors.

Five years later, our dominance in electrical appliances disappeared as stereos, televisions, microwave ovens and other goods flooded in from Japan and other Far Eastern countries. This time we blamed our losses on dumping and copying of our products.

In 1980, when the pride of our manufacturing prowess, the automotive industry, was clearly in jeopardy, we began to realize that the problem was truly serious. While we found additional reasons to explain our problems, concern about our competitiveness was now becoming widespread.

We thought we still had security in high technology and new product development. Now we know that even these niches are not safe. In 1985 we lost our leadership in the production of microchips, the very heart of the information age. Signs now indicate that the aerospace industry will be the next place where we lose our leadership position. Even the warm security blanket of the Department of Defense will probably be insufficient to protect this industry beyond 1990.

In 15 short years we have seen an unprecedented change in a host of industries from smokestack to high tech. The ramifications for our economic well-being and standard of living have just started to be felt. It's time we realized that this sharp shift is not the result of trivial causes or the excuses we have used. It's because of an unprecedented race in all aspects of manufacturing. Let's examine just a few to understand the accelerating pace of the race for a competitive edge.

ARE WE LOSING THE RACE?

- ● 1970—Smokestack

- ● 1975—Appliance

- ● 1980—Automotive

- ● 1985—Electronics

- ● 1990 (?)—Aerospace

2:   THE DRIVE FOR QUALITY

Quality is probably the best aspect of the race that enables us to understand its impact on the marketplace. Until 1970, we used the word yield as the measure of quality. Our concentration was on how many good parts resulted from the material we put into the plant. This terminology indicates that probably more than 10% of the parts were scrapped. Now we use the word yield only when referring to the start-up of new processes and products where we know that initial losses will be high.

During the 70s our terminology changed. We adopted the word scrap to denote the shift in our focus from good parts to defective ones. Improvement occurred and our losses dropped below 10%. In 1980 we realized that even this improved level of quality was insufficient. We began to lose markets because our competitors supplied products of superior quality. The Japanese penetration of the American automotive industry is a classic example. Consumers were initially attracted by the promise of low-cost, economical transportation. Once they became accustomed to the quality and dependability of Japanese cars, a new standard was set in the marketplace. The American automotive companies lost market share because of lower quality and soon realized that improving it was essential if they wanted to remain in business. Slogans like "Quality is number one" and "Quality is job one" appeared on the scene, signifying the drive to reduce scrap below 1%.

Now our terminology has changed once again to reflect the even higher level of quality that the market is demanding. We have started to talk again in terms of "zero defects. " The magnitude of this change is seen in the new unit of measurement introduced by the Japanese to gauge progress toward this goal—parts per million scrap. Parts per million means that our quality goal has increased four orders of magnitude in the last 15 years. We are seeing an unprecedented acceleration in the race for higher quality. But quality is not the only aspect of the race.

QUALITY

- **Before 1970 —Yield (Defects: ~ 10%)**

  - **1970 —1980 — Scrap (Defects: < 10%)**

    - **1980 —"Quality is number 1" (Defects: < 1%)**

      - **1985 —Zero Defects (Defects: parts per million)**

3: PRODUCT LIFE CYCLES SHRINK

Consumers have not only been insisting on higher quality, but they are also voraciously consuming new products. Prior to 1970, we were accustomed to buying products that changed only slightly each decade. As we moved into the 70s, new products entered and were accepted in the marketplace at an increasingly faster rate.

We experienced the dizzying pace of change as electronics were introduced into previously staid products like watches and calculators. We moved from an era where a good watch not only lasted a lifetime, and was even passed on to the next generation, to a disposable world where we purchase new watches with every improvement in technology or change in fashion. Calculators changed from bulky mechanical and electrical machines with limited capability to miniaturized electronic marvels rivaling earlier computers. Instead of being limited to offices, calculators are now found in almost every purse, billfold and schoolbag. The engineer's slide rule has become a museum piece.

The shortening of product life cycles was not confined just to consumer products. Every industrial organization has been impacted. Even a time-honored product like the 2 x 4 is being replaced by galvanized steel structurals in many buildings. The pressure for new products could not be supported by our conventional design methods. We had to develop computer-aided design and computer-aided engineering systems to cope with an ever-increasing pressure for new products. By 1980, the demands of the market and increased capabilities of our design processes shortened life cycles to just a few years.

Today we are in a period where, if a company is late to the marketplace with a new product by six or nine months, it runs the risk of losing the entire market. Certainly the life cycle of most products has shrunk again. We can only guess the life cycle of products today. We will know tomorrow.

PRODUCT LIFE CYCLES

● **1970—Decade(s)**

    ● **1975—Many Years**

        ● **1980—A Few Years**

            ● **1985—?**

4: AUTOMATING OUR PLANTS

This race for a competitive edge is also manifested in ways less obvious to the typical consumer. Machine technology has been changing at an explosive rate. Prior to the 70s, we used conventional electromechanical equipment that had changed little in the last 40 or 50 years. By 1975 we had introduced computer technology into production operations in the form of numerically-controlled (NC) equipment.

At that time we might have logically projected that the adoption of this new technology would take decades, since it involved very large investments and a substantial retraining of the work force. Remember, it was the first time we introduced computers and programming onto the shop floor. Nevertheless, this technology is commonplace today.

By 1980, even before NC technology was widespread, we had introduced the next generations—CNC (Computer Numerically Controlled) and DNC (Direct Numerically Controlled) equipment. Instead of stand-alone NC machines, we now had cells, or groups of machines, interlinked and controlled from a single computer source. Despite this rapid change, by 1985 we were forced to invest additional huge sums to follow the Japanese in the introduction of Flexible Manufacturing Systems (FMS) . Changing markets and management perceptions demanded *flexible* computer-controlled equipment capable of handling small-lot production, and rapidly changing product designs.

Even while we are still investing in FMS we can see the next step around the corner. Many major manufacturers are already investing tens of millions of dollars in the attempt to build totally automated factories, the lightless plants, a technology which even today is unclear in its design and usage.

Everyone is taking tremendous risks in the attempt to participate and not fall behind in this race. The pressures to gain a competitive edge through machine technology are great, but they are even more intense and obvious in the frantic attempts to find a better logistical system to run our plants.

MACHINE TECHNOLOGY

- 1970—Conventional Machines

- 1975—Numerically Controlled (NC) Machines

- 1980—Cells of Computerized (NC) Machines

- 1985—Semi-Automated Plants

- 1990 (?)—Lightless Plants

5: LOGISTICS TO SPEED THE FLOW OF MATERIALS

During the 40s, 50s, and into the 60s, we used manual "order point" techniques to control the ordering and flow of material in our plants and warehouses. This was our logistical system. About 1965, we tried for the first time to tap the power of the computer for this task through a technique called Materials Requirements Planning (MRP) . Despite an investment estimated at $10 billion, we were not satisfied with the results. In 1975 we renamed it closed loop MRP, believing that feedback on the status of shop orders and purchase orders was the key to faster material flow. In 1980, it was MRP II, an effort to get the entire manufacturing organization—marketing, engineering, manufacturing and finance—singing off the same hymn sheet.

Each phase of our MRP journey involved large investments in computers, software and training in how we managed our businesses. It's been estimated that we've spent more than $30 billion, but even these enhancements and investments were not enough. MRP did not enable us to maintain leadership in the race for a competitive edge. The Japanese approach to the logistics of the shop floor, Just-in-Time/Kanban, proved superior to our efforts. Today some Western companies are attempting to emulate them. Meanwhile the Japanese and others are searching frantically for an even better system, called synchronized manufacturing, even though we have yet to define exactly what it is.

LOGISTICAL SYSTEMS

● 1950—Order Point

  ● 1965—MRP

    ● 1975—Closed Loop MRP

      ● 1980—MRP II

        ● 1985—Synchronized
                    Manufacturing

6: INVENTORY TURNS MEASURE PERFORMANCE

Nowhere has the race manifested itself more than in inventory turns. The rate of turnover or usage of inventory is an excellent measure of the performance and rate of change of manufacturing companies. During the 70s the acceptable standard for inventory turnover was somewhere between two and five a year. A study by the international consulting firm of Booz, Allen & Hamilton showed that U. S. firms averaged 3.7 turns during the 70s. The Japanese average, while higher, was still only 5.5. These were the standards. Those with the foresight and courage to suggest that double-digit turns were possible were labeled as lunatics.

In the current decade, two to five inventory turns is considered totally inadequate. The standard of acceptable performance has shifted dramatically in just a few years to somewhere between five and 20. Inventory turns of two digits that were considered to be impossible just a few years ago are now a must. A number of western companies already are operating in the range of 30 to 80 inventory turns. Some Japanese companies (thank heaven there are only a few) have demonstrated that inventory turns of three digits can be achieved. Everywhere there is a drive to do much, much better than was previously thought possible.

Even with these dramatic new, and as of yet generally unreached goals, another new target is emerging on the horizon—negative inventory turns. Turning inventory so rapidly that we are paid for the finished product before we have to pay for the raw materials is now considered a possibility. We're probably already paying for the hamburger we buy at a fast food store before they have to pay for the meat. Maybe it's also possible in a manufacturing company. It's quite a change when inventory is viewed as a source rather than as a user of money.

INVENTORY TURNS

● **Before 1980 — 2-5**

  ● **After 1980 — 5-20**

    ● **1985 — Some already at 30-80**

      ● **1985 (JAPAN) — A few have demonstrated > 100**

        ● **Tomorrow (?) — Negative Inventory Turns**

7: THE RACE FOR A COMPETITIVE EDGE IS ACCELERATING—RAPIDLY

These few examples illustrate that the race for the competitive edge is clearly intensifying. The challenge that the Western manager faces is how to become much more competitive very quickly. We have entered a period unlike any since the days of the industrial revolution. The implications for companies, countries and our standard of living are every bit as profound as when the first industrial companies began to appear in England years ago.

It is no longer a question of a cycle of good times and bad. We cannot batten down the hatches and hope to survive, as if this were another passing storm. We can no longer use the conventional approach of cutting expenses and firing people in the bad times. We must find a way to continually improve—in good times and bad. We must choose to be in the competitive edge race. The companies that elect to shrink in order to pass the bad times will simply disappear. The ones that survive will be those companies that will find a way to participate in this ever-increasing competitive edge race.

The magnitude of our problem is revealed once we accept that we are behind and recognize that we have only a little time left. Our resources, particularly management, are severely limited, and our funds are not sufficient to allow us risky experiments. We must make the correct decisions this time or be prepared to live with the consequences.

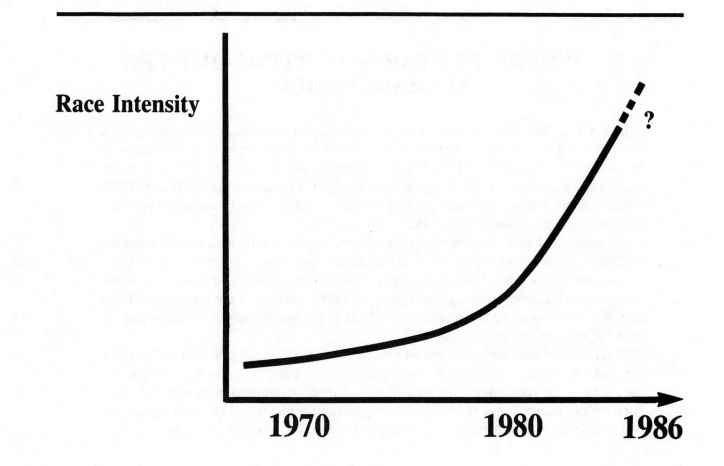

Race Intensity

1970   1980   1986

How to become more competitive considering

- **Limited time**

- **Limited resources**

- **Limited funds**

8: WHERE TO START—SORTING OUT THE ALPHABET SOUP

In the last five years, a host of new and powerful techniques have emerged as possible solutions. A whole lexicon of new terms has been developed that seems to be characterized by two- and three-letter abbreviations. We are urged to implement statistical process control (SPC), group technology (GT), factories of the future (FOF) and on and on. The Western manager is challenged to solve a very fundamental problem from this alphabet soup of solutions.

To understand each of these new technologies can, by itself, be a time-consuming challenge. Deciding which are best is a formidable task. Figuring out how to put them all together seems beyond our reach. Since we don't have the time, resources or funds to do everything, everywhere, we had better be convinced that we are taking the actions that will leapfrog us back into the race. There is no longer margin for error and no time for risky experiments.

What are the most important steps to take first and which technologies will give us the greatest return so we have the time and funds to implement the rest? Maybe we should begin by reexamining the goal of this race. By coming to grips with the basic purpose and nature of our manufacturing organizations maybe we can find a path that will enable us both to participate in and win the race for a competitive edge.

GROUP-TECHNOLOGY

COMPUTER INTEGRATED MANUFACTURING

ZERO-INVENTORY

STATISTICAL PROCESS CONTROL

JUST-IN-TIME

U-CELL

THE COMPETITIVE EDGE RACE: WHERE DO WE START?

CAD/CAM

SYNCHRONIZED MANUFACTURING

ROBOTICS

QUALITY CIRCLES

FACTORY OF THE FUTURE

ZERO-DEFECT

9:   WHAT IS THE GOAL OF THE RACE?

What are we really trying to accomplish in our businesses? Did the investors and employees put their money and efforts into the company with the altruistic intent of providing·better service to their customers? Or did they do it because they wanted the prestige of having the largest market share? Did they want to boast that they had lower costs than their competitors? Was the goal of these investors and employees to enjoy the pride of having the highest quality products? Is it likely that they invested their money and efforts to build the company just in order to have it survive?

We think not. All of these targets may be useful means to the goal of the company, but they themselves are not the goal. We believe that the goal of a manufacturing company is one and only one—to make money in the present as well as in the future. That is what winning the race is all about. But what does "making money" really mean?

WHAT IS THE GOAL?

Better Customer Service?
Larger Market Share?
Lower Cost?
High Quality?
Survival?

⬇

Make MONEY in the present as well as in the future

⬇

Win the race

10: "MAKING MONEY"—HOW DO WE MEASURE IT?

We all know the bottom line measurements of making money. A company needs to make a net profit, an absolute measurement of making money. But is this measurement by itself sufficient? If a company made $10 million, is that good or bad? If they had invested $20 million, it's quite good. But if the investment were $200 million, it's lousy. We need an additional measurement that shows how much money we made relative to the money we invested in the business, a measure like return on investment. These two measurements seem sufficient, but many a company has been rudely reminded by the threat of bankruptcy, that there is also a survival measurement, like cash flow. Cash flow is an on-off measurement. When we have enough cash, it is not important. When we don't have enough cash, nothing else is important.

While these three bottom line measurements are sufficient to determine when the business is making money, they are woefully inadequate to judge the impact of specific actions on our goal. For example, in what size batches should we process material through our plants? Five? Fifty? Maybe five hundred? How will these batch sizes impact the bottom line of the entire company? Or, should we buy a new robot? It certainly is going to be more efficient, but it is also expensive. What will be the resulting impact on our financial measures? Or should we accept an order for a product when the selling price is substantially below our standard price? We clearly need some type of bridge between the specific operational decisions we must make and the bottom line measurements of the entire company.

Today, our bridge is based on the cost concept. We have developed a host of procedures and systems based on the idea of cost. We employ the technique of economic order quantities to help determine batch sizes. We analyze investment opportunities based on cost reduction to determine where to employ our capital. We calculate product costs and margins to help understand which products we should push in the market and which we should discontinue.

The cost concept and cost procedures are the current bridge between our actions and the bottom line measurements, but is this bridge taking us in the right direction?

THE GOAL: TO MAKE MONEY

Bottom line measurements

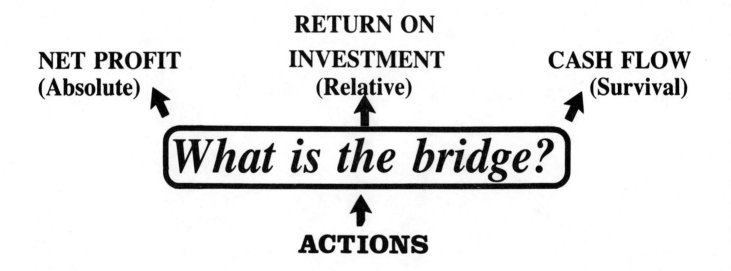

NET PROFIT
(Absolute)

RETURN ON
INVESTMENT
(Relative)

CASH FLOW
(Survival)

What is the bridge?

ACTIONS

11: IS THE COST BRIDGE FATALLY FLAWED?

Despite the fact that cost procedures are well defined, managers commonly override the calculated results because of their experience and intuition. Economic order quantities are ignored. Instead of using the calculated lot size of 46. 5, we chose 50 and then override this decision when we split and overlap batches in our plants. Major investments are currently being made in factories of the future where the projected return on investment is seven or eight years even though our required return for other investments is less than three years. We decide that factories of the future are strategically important regardless of what the cost calculations show. Orders are accepted by plants even though they shouldn't be according to cost recommendations.

Currently we are using both cost and intuition to determine what actions to take. The mere fact that we override the cost recommendations so frequently already tells us that cost procedures are not adequate. Intuition often helps to improve the cost recommendation, but unfortunately intuition is not a basis for good communication. Even though this combination of cost and intuition were not sufficient in the past, this new competitive race has now made them totally obsolete, as can be seen by the next two examples.

THE BRIDGE:

Currently we are using cost (+ intuition).

Is it good enough in this new competitive world?

12: THE COST CONCEPT BLOCKS BETTER QUALITY

The competitive edge race is forcing us to reduce scrap to improve quality. Suppose a company saves $10,000 a year in labor and material every time it reduces scrap by 1%. If the scrap level was 5% and the company was able to double the quality level by reducing scrap to approximately 2%, the savings would be $30,000 a year. Let's assume that the investment in equipment, tools or education required to achieve this improvement was $20,000. The return on this investment would be less than one year and the cost judgment would be to do it.

Let's see how the use of this cost bridge impacts the ever-increasing steps to improve quality in the race for "zero defects." Doubling quality again by further reducing scrap from 2% to 1% would result in a savings of only $10,000. The investment required now is undoubtedly higher than $20,000 since the first step probably required resolution of only one or two major problems while this step may involve several investments to resolve many smaller problems. Nevertheless, let's assume that the investment is still only $20,000. The decision now is less clear since two years are required to recover our investment.

The savings from a third doubling of quality by a scrap reduction from 1% to 0. 5% will only be $5,000. Our investment most certainly will be much larger than $20, 000, but let's be very conservative and again use this amount. Now the cost judgment will clearly be don't do it since the four-year return does not justify the investment.

How can we hope to reach a quality level of parts per million scrap when the cost bridge already blocks us around the 1% level? We know that when we produce defective products we don't just scrap material and labor, we are also scrapping our market. In our increasingly competitive world, we are forced to declare that "quality is number one," which means that every investment that involves quality improvement is allowed. We have totally lost the yardstick. The bridge in this area simply no longer exists.

The same cost judgment phenomenon that helped us in the past, and now blocks us from participating in the race, is also revealed in the frantic attempts to reduce inventory.

The cost concept blocks us from achieving a competitive edge through parts-per-million quality.

Reducing Scrap From To		Annual Cost Savings	Investment Needed	The Cost Judgment
5%	2%	$30,000	$20,000	Do
2%	1%	$10,000	$20,000	Indifferent
1%	0.5%	$5,000	$20,000	Do NOT Do

13:   HIGH INVENTORY TURNS AREN'T COST JUSTIFIED

Suppose a company has an inventory of $15 million and estimates the cost of carrying inventory at about 25% of its value. If the company is currently turning its inventory three times a year and is able to double the turnover to six, costs will be reduced by approximately $2 million a year (25% x $15 million/2) . Such an inventory reduction is not achieved without efforts and investment. If the investment needed is around $2 million, then the cost judgment will be to do it since the return is approximately one year.

The situation changes when the company wishes to double inventory turns once again from six to twelve. Now the cost savings are only $1 million (25% x $15 million/4) . The investment required is probably higher. Nevertheless, even if we use the same $2 million, the decision now is unclear because the payback is over two years. The cost judgment is neutral. If there are some good intangible reasons for investing, do it. If there aren't, don't. But when the company is taking the necessary step for survival in this new competitive race and attempts to double inventory turns from 12 to 24, it is blocked. The cost savings are now only $500,000, a four-year return. Now the cost judgment is loud and clear. Don't do it.

It is very obvious that we must look for a better bridge to guide us in our efforts to catch up. Fortunately, there is a widely used set of three measurements that are not bottom line measurements and not cost measurements. These measurements are total sales, total inventory and total operating expenses. The use of these measurements is widespread because our intuition is already telling us that they are a sound bridge. However, to use this throughput-inventory-operating expense bridge for specific decisions we need to develop procedures to guide our actions. As a first step in this process we should define precisely what we mean by throughput, inventory and operating expense.

The cost concept blocks us from achieving competitive edge through high inventory turns.

Increasing Inventory Turns		Cost Savings Per Year*	Investment Needed	The Cost Judgment
3	6	$2M	$2M	Do
6	12	$1M	$2M	Indifferent
12	24	$0.5M	$2M	Do NOT Do

*Assuming starting inventory of $15M and 25% carrying cost

14: THROUGHPUT-INVENTORY-OPERATING EXPENSE—A BETTER BRIDGE

We have chosen to define these three measurements in the following way:

Throughput - The rate at which an organization generates money through sales. Notice, through sales, not through production. If we have produced something and haven't sold it, it's not throughput.

Inventory - All the money that the system invests in purchasing things that it intends to sell. This definition of inventory deviates from traditional definitions since it excludes the added value of labor and overhead. We have elected to use this definition in order to eliminate the distortions and counter-productive decisions caused by accounting-generated inventory profits and inventory losses.

Operating Expense - All the money the system spends in order to turn inventory into throughput. This definition of operating expense includes not just direct labor, but also management, computers, and even the secretaries. If a secretary's job is not to assist in turning inventory into throughput, then her salary is not a real operating expense, but just a waste.

A much broader explanation of the meaning of these measurements can be found in *The Goal - A Process of Ongoing Improvement*. We call these three measurements the global operational measurements. The first step in using them as a bridge is to clarify the linkages between these operational measurements and the bottom line financial measurements.

THE COST CONCEPT MUST BE REPLACED BY GLOBAL OPERATIONAL MEASURES.

THROUGHPUT—
The rate at which the system generates money through sales.

INVENTORY—
All the money the system invests in purchasing things the system intends to sell.

OPERATING EXPENSE—
All the money the system spends in turning inventory into throughput.

15: T-I-OE AND THE BOTTOM LINE

We know that our goal is to make money and that we measure progress toward it by the three bottom line financial measurements. If we take actions that increase these three measures simultaneously we are certainly moving in the right direction.

The intuitively felt connection between throughput-inventory-operating expense (T-I-OE) and the bottom line measures are sharpened with our new definitions. Now we can see that when throughput is increased without adversely effecting inventory and operating expense, then net profit, return on investment and cash flow are simultaneously increased. We achieve the same result when operating expense is decreased without an adverse affect on throughput or inventory.

When we analyze the impact of reducing inventory we see that the result is not the same. Decreasing inventory directly increases only return on investment and cash flow. It does not have any direct impact on net profit. Should we conclude that inventory is less important than throughput and operating expense? That seems to be the way we have regarded it.

It's also the way most managers have historically viewed T-I-OE. Net sales (throughput) and total operating expense have always been seen to be important. Inventory has frequently taken a back seat. When we look more closely, we see that inventory does impact net profit and also has an additional effect on the other two bottom line measurements. However, these impacts are indirect—through the carrying charge channel.

THE DIRECT IMPACT: OPERATIONAL MEASUREMENTS AND THE BOTTOM LINE

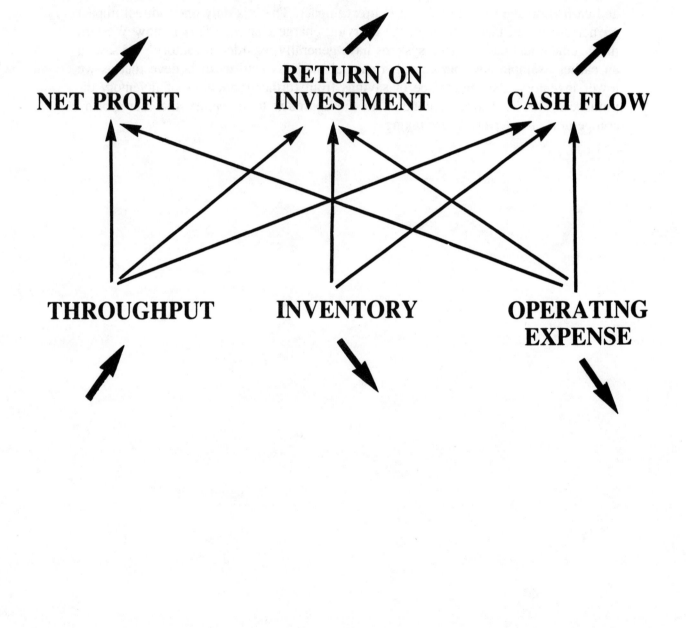

16: INVENTORY AND THE CARRYING CHARGE CHANNEL

The indirect impact of inventory on the three bottom line measurements is typically estimated through the use of carrying charges. We recognize that lowering inventory reduces a number of operating expenses, such as interest charges, storage space, scrap, obsolescence, material handling and rework. Recently most companies have been estimating their annual carrying charges to be some number around 25% of the value of the inventory (value including labor and overhead) . Since reducing inventory lowers operating expense, it increases the three bottom line measurements.

We can now see that reducing inventory has a twofold impact on return on investment and cash flow due to its direct and indirect impact. There is only one indirect impact on net profit and that is through the carrying charge channel. This is how Western management and our financial systems have generally regarded inventory. We saw in an earlier example how our current financial methods lead us to believe that as we lower inventory, the importance of savings from further reductions of inventory diminishes. This is in drastic contrast to the approach to inventory that our worthy competitors, the Japanese, are taking.

THE INDIRECT IMPACT: INVENTORY AND CARRYING CHARGES— THE WESTERN VIEW

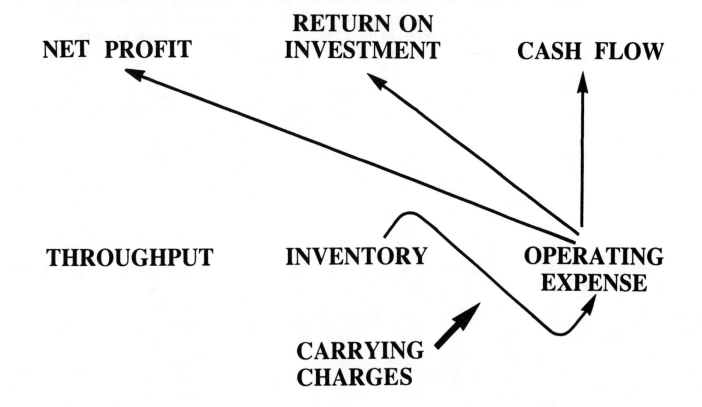

17: WHO IS RIGHT—OUR FINANCIAL SYSTEMS OR THE JAPANESE?

The Japanese place enormous emphasis on reducing inventory. In fact, they go to such an extreme that they characterize inventory as "an evil." They make tremendous efforts to reduce inventory no matter how small it is already. The Japanese approach has recently been advocated in the USA by the American Production and Inventory Control Society (APICS) under the name of "zero inventory" to illustrate this all-consuming drive to eliminate inventory.

If you had to decide which is right, our financial systems or the Japanese, what would be your choice? We, like you, believe the Japanese probably are right. We believe that there is a second indirect impact of inventory, one that is not yet recognized by our financial systems.

There is a growing awareness in Western industry that there are "intangible" benefits from reducing inventory, which in this frantic race are more important than anything else. We are increasingly recognizing that inventory has significant impact on our competitive position in the market. In order to clarify this impact, we should examine the elements that compromise competitiveness in the market.

The traditionally recognized impact of inventory improvements diminishes rapidly as inventory decreases.

So why do the Japanese place so much emphasis on inventory reduction?

The Japanese approach is advocated in the USA under the name

"ZERO-INVENTORY."

18: THE SIX COMPETITIVE EDGE ISSUES

We can gain a competitive edge by having better products, lower prices or faster response. Oddly enough, each of these categories can be separated into two distinct branches. A competitive edge can be gained through our products by both superb quality and excellent engineering. For example, suppose that two companies are offering the market the same product for the same price, but one of them produces a much better quality product. Certainly, the company with superior quality will eventually capture the market. We are already well aware of one startling example—Japanese cars. The Japanese have penetrated Western markets because of their superb quality and not because of more features or faster delivery. On the other hand, we can gain a competitive edge because our products are better engineered than our competitors. If two companies offer the market the same type of product at the same price and quality, then the company that offers more product features will certainly capture the market.

The same pattern holds true where price is concerned. The company with the highest margins (lowest cost) will have more flexibility on pricing and thus can capture the market. But we shouldn't ignore the tremendous advantage in lower investment per unit. This competitive edge also gives a company greater flexibility to compete because of its lower break-even point.

Responsiveness is likewise composed of two parts. The first is the competitive advantage stemming from better due-date performance. We promise to deliver a certain quantity of product by a certain date. How many times do we succeed in fulfilling this commitment? If we accomplish it 80% of the time while our competitor's performance is consistently 90%, he will eventually get our customers. If we are delivering as promised 90% of the time and our competitor's performance is 95%, he will still win. It is a never-ending race since customers are constantly increasing their expectation levels, always adjusting to the high performer as the standard.

Due-date performance differs from shorter-quoted lead times, the second responsiveness avenue. This advantage gives us the ability to commit to an earlier delivery than our competitors. Every salesman has learned the significant advantage in offering the client fast deliveries.

We believe that these six elements comprise the competitive edge issues in today's and tomorrow's market. The real race today is not just on one of them, but on all six. Oddly enough, most of these elements are considered by our financial systems as intangibles. Maybe they should be thought of instead as our future throughput. We are going to show, through a simple example, the real impact of inventory on our future throughput and the six competitive edge elements.

A ROLE FOR REDUCED INVENTORY?

PRODUCT
- QUALITY
- ENGINEERING

PRICE
- HIGHER MARGINS
- LOWER INVESTMENT PER UNIT

RESPONSIVENESS
- DUE-DATE PERFORMANCE
- SHORTER QUOTED LEAD TIME

19: A HIGH INVENTORY ENVIRONMENT

We can explore the impact inventory has on the six competitive edge elements by contrasting a high inventory manufacturing environment with a low inventory one. Suppose a company had an order for 1,000 units which are manufactured in a five-step process. In high inventory manufacturing, the material might be processed and moved through the plant in a single batch of 1,000 pieces. Each operation completes all its work before any of the material is moved to the next operation. As material is released into the plant, the work-in-process inventory level rises and does not begin to decline until the product is completed at the last operation and can be shipped.

In this high inventory example, it takes about four months to complete the order even if we run the plant 24 hours a day, seven days a week. This is in marked contrast to low inventory manufacturing as we shall see.

HIGH-INVENTORY MANUFACTURING

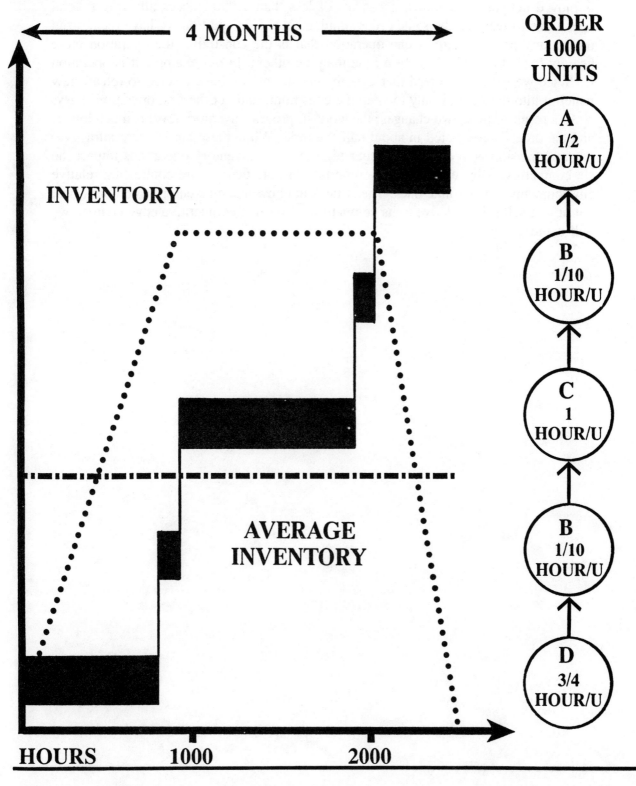

4 MONTHS

ORDER 1000 UNITS

INVENTORY

AVERAGE INVENTORY

HOURS 1000 2000

A
1/2
HOUR/U

B
1/10
HOUR/U

C
1
HOUR/U

B
1/10
HOUR/U

D
3/4
HOUR/U

20: A LOW INVENTORY ENVIRONMENT

In our low inventory manufacturing example, there are only two changes. First we have split and overlapped the batches. We no longer wait until each operation has completed the entire order before moving completed parts to the next operation. Material is moved between operations in batches of less than 1,000 pieces allowing several operations to work on the same order simultaneously. In addition we have recognized that in any process there is one operation that is the constraint, the operation more heavily loaded or that takes more time than the others. In our example it is operation C. Since we have recognized that C is the constraint, we have elected to release raw material into the process only to keep the constraint, and not the first operation, busy.

As a result of these two changes, the work-in-process inventory level is much lower, and the order is completed in about half the time. While these benefits are attractive, our real mission is to explore how our high and low inventory operations impact the six competitive edge elements. It's important to note that we are contrasting relative environments, not absolute ones. The issue is not how much inventory a company has, but how much it has relative to its competitors. The first competitive edge element we will explore is quality.

LOW-INVENTORY MANUFACTURING

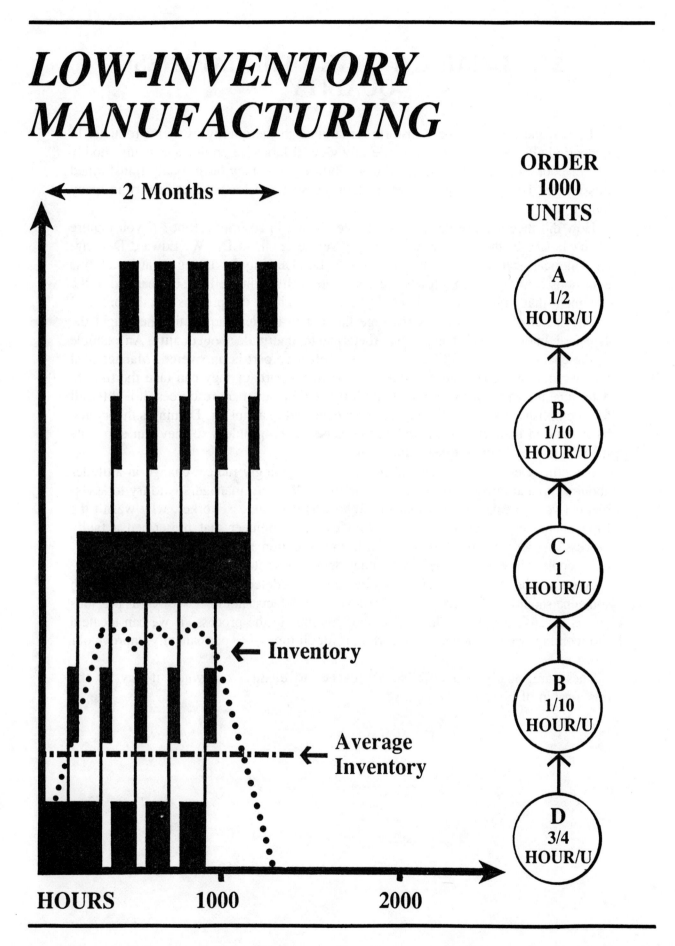

ORDER 1000 UNITS

2 Months

HOURS   1000   2000

Inventory

Average Inventory

A 1/2 HOUR/U

B 1/10 HOUR/U

C 1 HOUR/U

B 1/10 HOUR/U

D 3/4 HOUR/U

21: DEMING TAUGHT THE JAPANESE QUALITY

The Japanese have made a historic turnaround in the quality of their products. In the period after World War II we generally viewed Japanese products as being shoddy and of poor workmanship. In just a few short decades, they have totally transformed this image. Today the Japanese are setting the standard for product quality in many industries.

How did they achieve such a remarkable change in so brief a time? If you inquire of the Japanese, they almost universally give the credit to Dr. W. Edward Deming, an American statistician. With apologies to Dr. Deming for trying to articulate his enormous contribution in a few words, his approach might well be summarized in the statement that "quality control should be used to check the process not the product."

The secret of Dr. Deming's message lies not in the techniques that he taught the Japanese, but in how he changed their focus and their attitude about quality. An example of the change in focus can be seen when a defective part is uncovered. Management has two options. They can expedite a replacement part, or they can take the time to determine the cause of the problem. With limited management resources, it is difficult to accomplish both tasks. The Japanese have elected to adopt Dr. Deming's theory and have focused their efforts on finding the cause of the problem so they can eliminate it forever. We continue to expedite.

Adopting Deming's approach also requires a seemingly radical change in attitudes about scrap and rework. So often the reaction of Western managers is to try to assess blame (we also call it responsibility) . Who was the careless worker, why wasn't the foreman paying closer attention, or who was the engineer that prescribed a faulty process? As long as this attitude exists, it will be extremely difficult to find the cause. Our people will cover up the cause rather than expose it.

Adopting the Deming approach requires treating a defect not as a problem for which someone should be blamed. Deming believes that defects should be viewed as precious jewels because they can help us find shortcomings in the process. If we can locate a shortcoming, we have a chance to correct it for all times—to permanently improve our process.

These are clearly two different approaches to quality, but what, if any, is the relationship of inventory to quality?

Quality

Product

Quality control should check the process, not the product.

—Dr. Deming

22:   LOW INVENTORY EQUALS HIGH QUALITY

Suppose in manufacturing the 1,000 -piece order, that the product is damaged at the first operation of our process? This defect will eventually be caught, but where? Where do we typically inspect our product? Unfortunately, often after the last operation. In the high inventory environment, the damage will have occurred two months earlier, making it very difficult to determine what caused the defect. Who can recall what the operating problems were two months ago? Even more importantly, we have great pressure to expedite additional parts because the order is now going to be very late. Where do you think management will devote their efforts, to expediting or finding and solving the problem?

In the low inventory environment when the damage is detected at the last operation, we are still producing the product at the first operation. We should be able to much more easily determine the cause of the problem. The pressure to devote extensive management time to expediting now almost disappears. We have detected the problem before the entire order was produced incorrectly. Fewer replacement parts are required and we can produce them much more quickly than in the high inventory environment even without resorting to expediting.

Management now has the time and ability to find and eliminate the cause of the problem—hopefully forever. It is probably not possible to have very high quality unless we have low inventories. Certainly, there is a clear correlation between the people who have the highest quality—the Japanese—and the people with the lowest inventory, also the Japanese. Do you think that this is just a coincidence?

We can see the link between inventory and quality. Does a similar one exist between inventory and product engineering?

HIGH VS. LOW INVENTORY SYSTEMS: QUALITY CONTROL

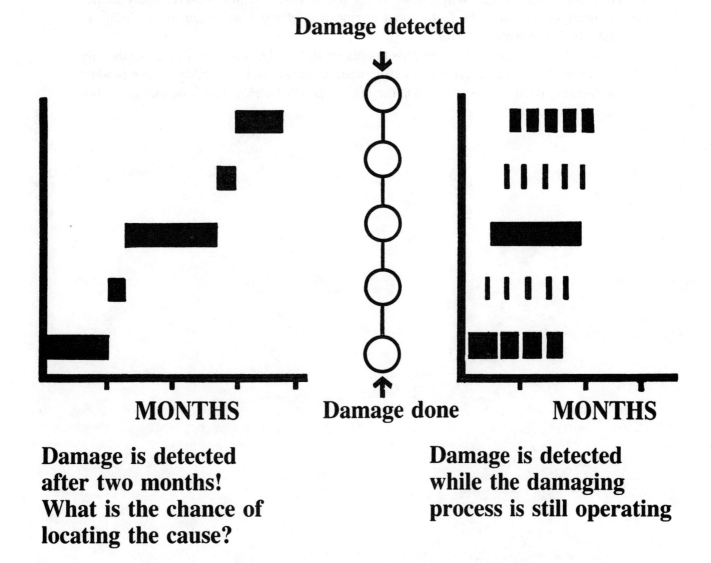

HIGH INVENTORY

LOW INVENTORY

Damage detected

MONTHS

Damage done

MONTHS

Damage is detected after two months! What is the chance of locating the cause?

Damage is detected while the damaging process is still operating

23: PRODUCT ENGINEERING AND INVENTORY—WHAT'S THE RELATIONSHIP?

The purpose of product engineering changes is to improve our products, to make them superior to those of our competitors. If we can offer products that have the latest functions and features desired by the marketplace we can gain a competitive edge. The power of new and better-engineered products is manifested in Wall Street's fascination with high tech companies. It is not the technology per se that draws investors but the potential of companies to be the first in the market with a new or improved product. If we can be the first out with a faster, cheaper personal computer, or a new biogenetic product, the world is our oyster.

Almost no sector of manufacturing is immune. Look at what has happened recently to once stable products like telephones, watches and even many industrial products. Being the first in the marketplace with an improved product is clearly an obvious competitive advantage. Why do we stress the obvious? Unfortunately, many manufacturing people have the feeling that engineering changes are often made simply to make their life more difficult.

The impact of engineering improvements on the market looks as if it depends only on our market research efforts to define market needs, and the ability of our product engineering departments to develop the needed products. How can it be that inventory has an impact here?

Product

Engineering

The purpose of engineering changes is to improve the product!

24: LOW INVENTORY, QUICKER NEW PRODUCT INTRODUCTION

Assume that an engineering change affecting the first operation is released one month after an order has been started in the plant. In high inventory manufacturing the first operation is already completed. The plant manager is faced with the choice of scrapping or reworking this material or delaying implementation of the engineering change until the next production order for this product. If we elect the latter choice it will be more than three months before we can provide the improved product to the marketplace. How many managers have the courage to scrap such an order and how many will choose to implement the engineering change with the next order? All of us know the answer.

In the low inventory environment, a portion of the order has not yet been processed through the first operation and will not require scrap or rework if we implement the engineering change. The superior product will be available to the market in less than two weeks. The company with the low inventory environment has the superior product available in the marketplace for a significant period without competition and should be able to gain additional sales and market share. As product life cycles are continually reduced, these effects become more and more important.

It is now quite obvious that inventory effects the competitive edge of the product, but how does inventory effect price in a more significant way than we already recognize through the carrying charge channel?

HIGH VS. LOW INVENTORY SYSTEMS: ENGINEERING CHANGES

HIGH INVENTORY

LOW INVENTORY

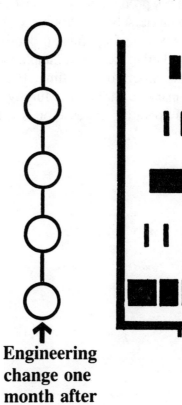

MONTHS

Engineering change one month after start of order.

MONTHS

Improved product will be available only several months after engineering change.

Improved product will be available in less than two weeks

25: MURPHY—VILLAIN OR EXCUSE?

Price is a well understood and sought after competitive advantage. The company with high margins has flexibility to selectively lower prices. Or it can use its high margins to gain a competitive edge in other ways such as increasing its sales force, advertising or product engineering. If we can become the low cost producer, we have a clear advantage. Unfortunately, there is often a big gap between planned and actual margins.

Murphy's Law (things will go wrong at the worst possible time) is well known in all our plants. No matter how well we plan, even when we build in large measures of safety, we still constantly expedite and expend lavish amounts of overtime in order to get orders shipped on time. This problem is so widespread that it's often referred to as the end-of-the-month syndrome. Somehow through special efforts we ship more than half the month's production in the last few days.

Whenever we find ourselves in trouble with shipping on time, whether it's the end-of-the-month or when an important order is due, we invariably turn to overtime, premium freight and other expensive, unplanned actions. The end result is that we may or may not get the orders out on time, but we certainly incur additional operating expense and our margins shrink. Is Murphy really the one causing these delays and thus the increased operating expense or is it the mode of high inventory that we are using?

Price $\diagup$ ***High Margins***

Plan, take safety measures, nevertheless, you will need overtime to finish the order on time.

—Murphy

26: HIGH INVENTORY—THE REAL CAUSE OF OVERTIME

There is no absolute measure of a high or low inventory environment. These are relative terms. We can only judge whether we have high or low inventory by looking at our competitors. If we have high inventory relative to our competitors, we will have long production lead times since work-in-process inventory and production lead time are really the same thing. If our competitors have lower inventory, our marketing people will probably be forced to promise deliveries in a shorter period than our normal lead time. Suppose marketing had to promise the order for delivery in three months, which is less than the four month production lead time of the high inventory company. Manufacturing will be forced into considerable overtime and possibly other additional costs in order to meet the delivery date.

In the low inventory environment, the production lead time is substantially shorter than the three months demanded by the marketplace, and no overtime will be needed even if Murphy does strike. Inventory is not generally recognized as causing overtime, but maybe it's the prime reason. In the defense industry the importance of inventory is generally downgraded because of government progress payments. Consequently work-in-process inventories are very large and production lead times are quite long. Nevertheless overtime is typically much higher than in almost any other industry.

The linkage of inventory and the competitive edge elements seems closer than we originally recognized. There certainly is also an impact of inventory on investment per unit, but is there also more than meets the eye?

HIGH VS. LOW INVENTORY SYSTEMS: HIGH MARGINS

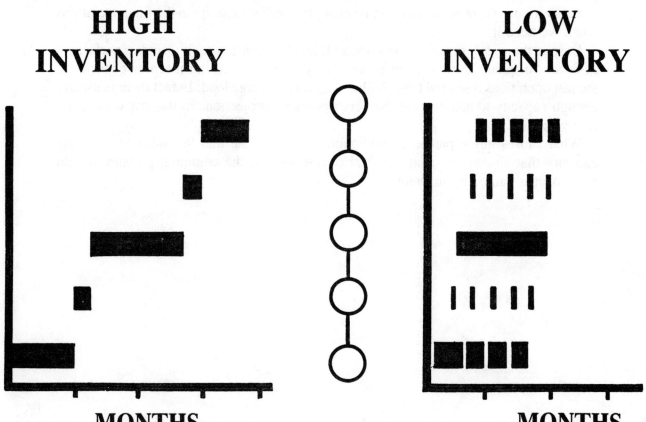

HIGH INVENTORY

LOW INVENTORY

MONTHS

MONTHS

Marketing had to promise the order in 3 months

The plant is forced into considerable overtime.

Plant production lead time is shorter than the lead time promised by marketing. No overtime will be needed.

27: DOES THE END-OF-THE-MONTH SYNDROME CAUSE THE PURCHASE OF EVEN MORE EXCESS CAPACITY?

Coping with the end-of-the-month syndrome is a major, ongoing problem for most plants. Every month, we encounter a surge of product at the final operations that must be processed in the last week of the month if we are to make our shipping goals. We start with liberal doses of overtime but find that it's often insufficient to handle this peak load. Next we find ourselves continually requesting additional equipment for these last operations. There never seems to be enough machine capacity in the final operations when we need it.

Despite the widely perceived need for additional machine capacity, studies performed in dozens of plants show that, in almost every case, the existing machine capacity of the last operations is several times higher than their average load. In fact there is usually enough capacity to handle even the very optimistic projections in the last year of the five-year forecast.

What causes this apparent contradiction? Is it possible that the substantial excess capacity that already exists at the final operations and the continual pressure to add more of it is caused by inventory?

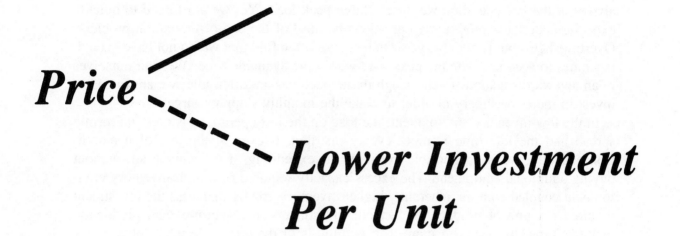

Price

*Lower Investment
Per Unit*

**We cannot finish the month because
the final operations are experiencing a peak
load . . . once again!**

We must buy more machines!

**—A common complaint
in almost any plant.**

28: HIGH INVENTORY MEANS EXTRA EQUIPMENT, SPACE AND INVESTMENT

In the high inventory environment the last operations are at peak load for an extended period and this peak load occurs at the worst possible time. When the material finally arrives at the last operation we have a large peak load. Yet we are forced to quickly expedite material through these operations because of the end-of-the-month problem. Overtime helps but is not always sufficient. We often find that we do not have enough machines to accommodate the peak load within the available time. We find ourselves in an awkward situation. Even though these machines are often idle, we are forced to invest in more machinery in order to make the monthly shipping targets.

In the low inventory environment, the load on the last operations is more uniformly spread and the idle time is more evenly distributed, even at the end of a month. Consequently, we are better able to handle the expediting, if it occurs at all, without buying additional equipment. The excess capacity required in a high inventory environment coupled with the inherently higher inventory greatly increases the investment required per unit of product. In fact our investments in inventories and production facilities typically comprise more than two-thirds of the total investment of a manufacturing company. In the low inventory environment the investment in equipment, facilities and inventory are much less and consequently the return-on-investment much higher. Even more importantly the break-even point is lower, enabling us to be much more flexible in pricing our products.

Do these intangible impacts of inventory also extend to the competitive edge of responsiveness? The general impression is that we should increase, not reduce, inventory in order to improve our responsivesness. Is it so?

HIGH VS. LOW INVENTORY SYSTEMS: INVESTMENT PER UNIT

HIGH INVENTORY

LOW INVENTORY

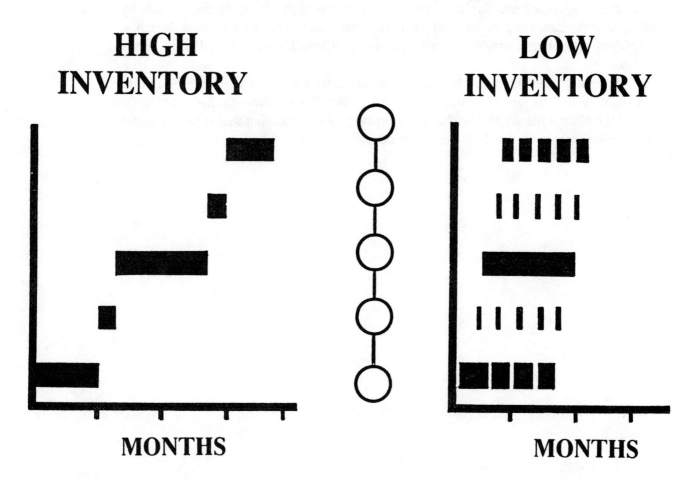

MONTHS

MONTHS

Last operation is at peak load for a long time. Pressure to ship the order may force plant to buy more machines which will not be utilized most of the time.

The load is more uniform at the last operation, no additional investment is required.

29: IS IMPROVING DUE-DATE PERFORMANCE BEYOND A PLANT'S CONTROL?

Almost every plant feels a need to improve its due-date performance. They also often feel helpless since they may lack control over the factors that cause them to miss due dates. It looks as if the major reasons for missing due dates are external to a plant. Either the vendors are unreliable or customers are constantly changing their minds by adding orders, canceling orders and changing due dates. One of the most common complaints of a plant manager is "just give me a reliable forecast and I'll ship things on time."

It's generally true that both of these conditions exist and heavily impact the ability of a plant to deliver on time. But does it mean that the solution to this problem is beyond the plant's reach? Maybe the real solution lies in something that is totally under the plant's control—its level of work-in-process inventory.

Due Date
Performance

Responsiveness

We miss due dates because our vendors are not reliable!

We miss due dates because our customers are constantly changing their minds!

—The two most common excuses.

30: LOW INVENTORY—THE KEY TO MORE ACCURATE FORECASTS

In order to understand the impact of work-in-process inventory on due dates we must examine something that looks at first glance as totally unrelated—the validity of our product forecast. Almost every plant has a forecast of demand which is quite reliable for some period of time into the future, then the validity of the forecast drastically deteriorates within a very short period of time. What causes this universal phenomenon?

If all companies in an industry are providing delivery of a product within two months, then customers will not place orders and commit themselves to specific due dates a year in advance. They probably will place their orders about 2 1/2 months before they need the product. Even when they place an order for a whole year, they will feel free to change the quantity and ship date two months in advance without risk of jeopardizing deliveries or placing their vendors in an impossible situation. Consequently, the plant's forecast for this product will be quite reliable for the first two months and quite unreliable for the period beyond three months. If we operate with high inventory relative to our competitors, it means that our production lead time is longer than the valid forecast horizon of the industry. The length of the valid horizon will be dictated by our low inventory competitors. As a result, the high inventory company's production plans are based on pure guesses and not on a reliable forecast.

It's no wonder that due-date performance is a problem where we have high inventories. When we operate in a lower inventory mode than our competitors, we enjoy an enviable position that gives us an inherently more accurate forecast. Now when we start production, we have firm orders or a valid forecast which is much less likely to change. Our due-date performance will certainly be much improved. Our production plans are now driven by more reliable information and we are in a much better position to give reliable requirements to our vendors. Remember, a prime reason that our vendors cannot deliver reliably is because we keep changing our requirements on them, the same way our customers are changing their requirements on us.

How about the last competitive element, shorter quoted lead times? Will we again find that inventory plays an unexpected role?

HIGH VS. LOW INVENTORY SYSTEMS: DUE DATE PERFORMANCE

HIGH INVENTORY

LOW INVENTORY

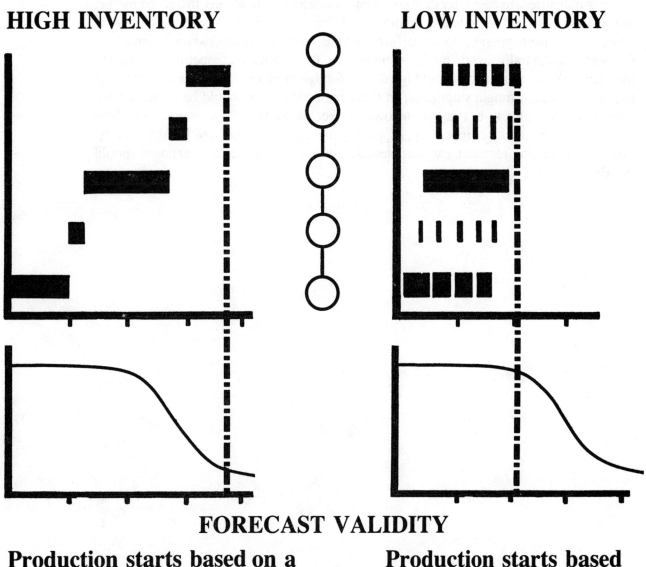

FORECAST VALIDITY

Production starts based on a guess. We oscillate between excess finished goods inventory and missed due dates.

Production starts based on good knowledge. Due date performance » 90%

31: SHORT LEAD TIMES—A KEY TO SURVIVAL?

Lead times are beginning to play an increasingly important role in the competitive edge race. An excellent example is the automotive industry's movement to just-in-time suppliers. If a vendor cannot learn how to supply the automotive assemblers just-in-time then they are not likely to remain a supplier for long. A pretty powerful reason for learning how to cut production lead times.

We have also seen the enormous power of shorter quoted lead times in a wide variety of other industries. In case after case companies have had dramatically increased market share when they had significantly shorter lead times than their competitors. In some cases, it has been possible to actually command premium prices when quoted lead times are substantially less than other competitors. This is a huge competitive advantage that many Western industries could have over foreign competitors because of the time required for ocean freight shipments. In these industries there should be no reason for a foreign competitor to beat us in our own market. It seems as if shorter quoted lead times should require more inventory, especially in work-in-process and finished goods. The less processing remaining to complete the product, the faster our response should be. But is it so?

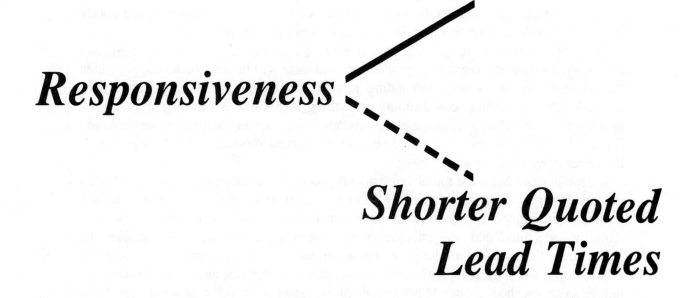

Responsiveness / *Shorter Quoted Lead Times*

My customers never complained about my quoted lead times until competition started an unfair war!

—The manager of a closed plant

32: INVENTORY LEVELS AND PRODUCTION LEAD TIMES ARE THE SAME THING

Production lead times and work-in-process inventory are really the same thing. One is a mirror image of the other. If we reduce work-in-process inventory, production lead times are reduced proportionately. What is not as well recognized is that finished goods inventory *should* be proportionate to work-in-process inventory.

Let's demonstrate it by an example. If a plant has one week of work-in-process inventory, then on the average its production lead time will be one week. Suppose that this plant is serving a very demanding market, a market that requires immediate deliveries. Since the plant could supply everything within one week, they should have about 1 to 1 1/2 weeks of finished goods inventory in order to meet customer demand. Some additional protection is needed beyond the normal production lead times due to the uncertainty of demand.

If another plant has three months of work-in-process inventory and is operating under the same market condition, it will be forced to hold nearly five months of finished goods. Some companies have demonstrated that it is possible to change a make-to-stock business into a make-to-order one by reducing production lead times sufficiently.

We stress the word *should* be proportionate to work-in-process inventories, and not is proportionate, since a reduction in work-in-process does not automatically cause a reduction in finished goods. Management must adjust their finished goods levels in accordance with any new level of work-in-process inventories to achieve these benefits. Thus responsiveness to the market demand is directly proportional to work-in-process inventory.

Since inventory impacts all six competitive edge elements, we are forced to conclude that the carrying charge channel is not the only indirect connection of inventory to the bottom line measurements. There must be another indirect linkage of inventory to our goal.

HIGH VS. LOW INVENTORY SYSTEMS: LEAD TIMES

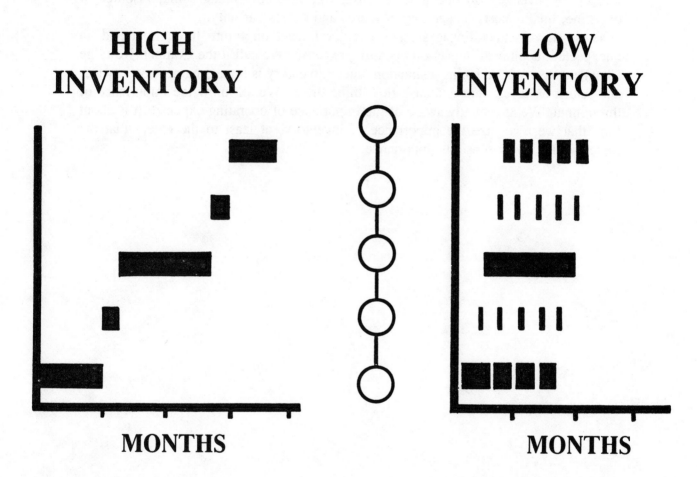

HIGH INVENTORY

LOW INVENTORY

MONTHS

MONTHS

Quoted lead times are long.

Lead times are much shorter.

- Production lead times are proportional to **work-in-process** inventory.
- Finished goods inventories should be proportional to production lead times.

33: INVENTORY AND FUTURE THROUGHPUT

Our analysis of the competitive edge elements illustrates how closely inventory is linked to sales (throughput) . Inventory should now be associated in our minds with future sales, with our ability to survive and thrive in tomorrow's markets. The more inventory that we are holding, the less promising will be the future. The less inventory that we hold today, the more secure our future is. We have also seen some unexpected impacts of inventory on operating expense, like inventory being a major source of overtime, quality costs, expediting expenses and excess capacity.

These new indirect linkages have a major impact on future throughput and an unexpected, additional impact on operating expense. We call it the Competitive Edge Channel. Now we are facing a situation where inventory is impacting net profit twice, and return on investment and cash flow three times. We all know the importance of throughput. We are equally aware of the importance of operating expense. It is about time that we recognize the importance of inventory, at least to the extent that the Japanese intuitively sense its importance.

THE COMPETITIVE EDGE IMPACT: OPERATIONAL MEASURES AND THE BOTTOM LINE

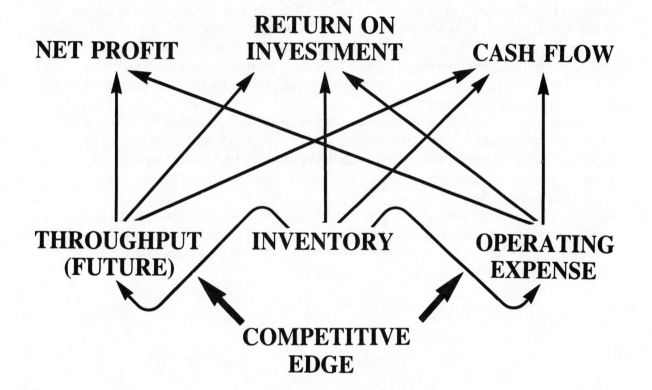

34: WHY INVENTORY IS A SECOND-CLASS CITIZEN

If there are so many obvious and important aspects of inventory to our competitive edge, there must be a very compelling and powerful reason why all companies are not currently operating in a low inventory mode. What causes so many plants to be at the other end of the inventory spectrum? The answer lies in our short-term view of the relative importance of throughput-inventory-operating expense and with the techniques available to manage the logistical flow of materials.

Every plant manager is painfully aware of the short-term importance of throughput and operating expense. He's often afraid that reducing inventory will adversely affect them. If a plant manager misses his shipping targets a couple of months in a row by as little as 10% the plant will probably lose money. The plant manager may be in deep trouble. Consequently, he's likely to keep lots of inventory just in case it's needed. His other concern is that if inventory is reduced too much, some operations might be starved for work, causing operating expenses to go up. Our performance measurements rivet our attention on these short-term measures, keeping inventory high and distracting us from their longer term importance.

Compounding our inattention to inventory has been the lack of effective logistical systems to drive inventory down without the risk of losing throughput or increasing operating expense. Consequently, we have traditionally clung to inventory as a security blanket to protect us against the complexities and disruptions of our plants and the vagaries of customer demand.

The frantic race for a competitive edge has changed all that. Currently, there is a frantic, worldwide search for an improved logistical system. A new buzz word, synchronized manufacturing, has been coined to encompass a yet undefined, better way to manage material flow.

The key to reduced inventory is synchronized manufacturing

. . . but what do we mean by this phrase?

35: WHAT IS SYNCHRONIZED MANUFACTURING?

Synchronized manufacturing is any systematic way that attempts to move material quickly and smoothly through the various resources of the plant in concert with market demand. The Japanese have used the example of a river system to characterize the smooth, even flow they are striving to achieve. Material should flow like brooks into streams, and streams into rivers and on and on without dams or disruptions interrupting the flow. There are a number of different types of logistical systems for planning and scheduling the procurement, production and distribution of materials. How can we find out if the Japanese example is sound, and which of the various available methods is best, and in what ways it is superior?

Let's try to approach this problem by using an analogy. We need an analogy that we can all relate to and that will enable us to express our dilemma of reducing work-in-process inventory without damaging throughput and operating expense. Once such an analogy is developed we will try to find a solution within the framework of the analogy. When an acceptable solution for the analogy is developed we will then transfer that solution into a plant environment and check its feasibility for reducing work-in-process inventory without harming throughput and operating expense. In this way it will be easier to examine the various logistical procedures and to compare them in a meaningful way.

The analogy that we have chosen is a troop of soldiers on a forced march.

FINDING A SOLUTION

Define an Analogy in which our problem can be easily expressed

⬇

Find a solution within the framework of the analogy

⬇

Transfer the solution to the plant environment

⬇

Check the feasibility of the solution

36: SPREADING TROOPS MEAN HIGH INVENTORIES

At first glance this seems to be a strange analogy, but a troop of soldiers on a forced march is remarkably similar to a manufacturing plant. We can view the first row of soldiers marching on the road as receiving raw material, virgin road, into the plant. This material is sequentially processed, walked on, by the subsequent rows of soldiers (production resources) . The last row releases (ships) the finished goods, road that the entire troop has walked on. Our troop uses production resources to receive raw materials, process them and produce a finished product—the same as a real plant.

In our analogy, work-in-process inventory is simply the distance between the first row of soldiers — those that convert raw material into work-in-process, and the last row which transfers the work-in-process into finished goods. When the troop starts its forced march, the soldiers are tightly bunched. But after only a few miles spreading is quite evident and continues to grow as the forced march continues. This spreading is a natural phenomenon which is found not only in our troop analogy, but also in activities as diverse as a funeral procession and a manufacturing plant. The spreading is caused by the combination of dependent events (activities that must be done sequentially) and statistical fluctuations. The spreading (inventory buildup) that occurs under these conditions can be demonstrated mathematically and is described in depth in THE GOAL.

The problem of reducing work-in-process inventory without jeopardizing throughput can be stated in our analogy as reducing the spreading of the troop without reducing its overall speed. What can we do to prevent the spreading of the troop without slowing down its overall movement? This is our problem.

A TROOP ANALOGY

MARCHING SOLDIERS

RAW MATERIAL →   **GOODS FINISHED** →

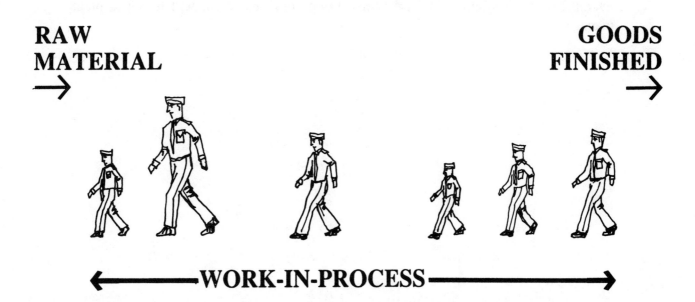

←————— **WORK-IN-PROCESS** —————→

Spreading troops mean high inventory. Closely packed troops mean lower inventory.

How can we prevent the troops from spreading?

37: REARRANGING THE SOLDIERS REDUCES SPREADING

Let's borrow an idea known by every experienced troop commander. If we put the slowest soldiers in the first row, followed by the next slowest soldiers in the second row, and so on until we have the strongest soldiers, those who are most able to run to close gaps, in the last row, we can reduce the spreading. In this way, whenever spreading occurs, the strongest soldiers (production resources) are positioned so that they can use their strength (extra capacity) to run and close the gaps (reduce work-in-process inventory) .

The throughput — the rate at which the troop as a whole is moving — is dictated, in any event, by the slowest soldier no matter where he is placed within the troop. Rearranging the soldiers in this sequence will reduce spreading without impacting the overall speed. This approach works for a troop commander but will it help a plant manager?

A TROOP ANALOGY

Put the slowest soldiers at the front and the strongest ones in the rear.

38:   A GOOD IDEA—BUT TOO EXPENSIVE

Transferring this solution into a plant environment means restructuring the plant so that the most heavily loaded resources (slowest soldiers) , the ones that can barely cope with the load, are the machines performing the first operations. Each subsequent operation would be done by the resource having the next least amount of excess capacity. If we were to restructure our plant in this way, the last operations would have the greatest amount of excess capacity. Any waves of inventory (spreading soldiers) that build up in the plant can be absorbed by the excess capacity of the upstream operations (the strong soldiers that can run to close up the gaps) .

It sounds like a good idea, but let's first estimate the cost, effort, time and chaos that will result from implementing such a plan. The results are intimidating. If we look further and consider that future changes in our product mix might alter the loads on our production resources, necessitating another restructuring of the plant, we are convinced that this is not a feasible solution. Our good idea has turned out to be very expensive and inflexible, so let's go back to our analogy and look for a more feasible solution. A word of warning — this solution looks appropriate when we are designing a new plant. Nevertheless, even in that case, there are much better solutions.

So we are back to the drawing board in our search for a better solution to our problem.

A TROOP ANALOGY

In other words, restructure your factory so that the most loaded machines (the primary capacity constraints) are at the first operations and have the machines with large excess capacity downstream.

Estimate the cost . . . and look for a more feasible solution.

39: DRUMMERS AND SCREAMING SERGEANTS

There is another way that a troop commander prevents his soldiers from spreading. He can put a drummer in the front row to set the pace or cadence for the troop. Whenever spreading occurs, the commander will have his sergeants shout at the appropriate soldiers to pick up the pace and close the gap. The drumbeat helps the troop to march in unison and coupled with the sergeant's expletives, limits the spreading.

The overall pace of the troop is dictated by the slowest soldier. If the slowest soldier can march to the drumbeat, then the spreading of the troops (buildup of work-in-process inventory) is contained without reducing the overall speed. Note that the drumbeat constrains the stronger soldiers from marching faster, even though they have the capacity to do so. Again, this approach works for the troop commander, but how can we use a drummer and shouting sergeants in our plants?

A TROOP ANALOGY

Put a drummer at the front to set the pace.

Have the sergeants constantly urge the soldiers to close any gaps.

40: EARMUFFS ON THE SOLDIERS

Using a drummer and sergeants in the plant initially seems strange, but isn't it really a common practice? The drummer is the materials or production control manager assisted by a computerized system. The sergeants are the expeditors. The drummer develops plans and schedules for when material should be procured and processed through the various production resources in order to meet customer requirements. The drumbeat is the production schedules dictating when and what material is supposed to be processed by each production resource. Expeditors are needed because orders are constantly behind schedule (unplanned work-in-process inventory — spreading) and we must push them to meet due dates — to close the gaps. Expeditors are, of course, not just people with this title, but frequently everyone in management.

It seems as if we are using this solution in our plants in the same way that it is used in the analogy, but is it so? What would you think of a commander who put earmuffs on the soldiers so they could not hear the drumbeat and then told each soldier to march at his maximum speed. The strong soldiers in the front lines will be forced to walk as fast as possible and cause spreading to occur between them and the weaker soldiers that follow. What would you think of such a commander?

It seems crazy but this is exactly what we are doing in our plants. Why would we do such a contradictory thing? The answer lies in attitudes that are deeply ingrained in our culture. What plant does not have the following motto:

A TROOP ANALOGY

That's common practice now:

The sergeant is the expeditor and the drummer
is the material management system assisted
by a computer.
But can the soldiers follow the drum beat?

41: "KEEP THE WORKERS BUSY"

"If a worker doesn't have anything to do, let's find him something to do."

It looks as if all our work ethic is based on this premise. In our plants this motto usually translates into giving a production worker more material to work on so he can produce additional products. Isn't that the same as putting earmuffs on the soldiers and causing each one of them to march as fast as he can even though it increases work-in-process inventory and doesn't increase throughput? In our plants, don't the use of efficiencies, piecework incentives and variances serve as the earmuffs on our workers. Let's examine this idea in more detail.

A TROOP ANALOGY

"If a worker doesn't have anything to do, let's find him something to do."

As long as this mentality exists, each soldier will proceed according to his potential and not according to the constraints of the troop.

Do efficiencies, incentives and variances allow your workers to follow the drum beat?

42: COULD HIGH EFFICIENCIES EVERYWHERE BE BAD?

Suppose that worker "X" is the slowest soldier and that this soldier is not in the first row. This means that "X" is fed material by a stronger soldier. Transferring this concept to our plant means that a bottleneck (X) is not at the first operation but is fed by some other non-bottleneck resource (Y) that has more capacity than the bottleneck. Our stronger soldier, the non-bottleneck, can produce more parts than the slowest soldier, the bottleneck, in the same time period.

Put yourself in the shoes of the foreman in charge of these non-bottleneck resources. If you are measured by "efficiency, " what will you encourage your workers to do? Work all the time so that your efficiencies will be very high! What will happen to these parts at the bottleneck? Won't they accumulate in front of it? Certainly a bad move from the point of view of the total plant. By attempting to be efficient we created more inventory (spreading) without gaining any additional throughput. But you shouldn't worry, the accumulation of the unneeded inventory will not occur in your deparment, but somewhere further along in the production process. You will be judged as doing a very good job—attaining very high efficiency from your workers.

One the other hand, if you try to do what is good for the plant as a whole you would restrict your workers to produce at the rate of the downstream bottleneck, which is less than their capacity. What will happen to your efficiency? Do you really think you will score high against your measurements? How do you think management will judge your performance if your department has low efficiencies? What would you choose if you were the foreman?

The same thing happens to a foreman in charge of non-bottleneck resources feeding parts to an assembly operation which also depends on parts that are in short supply. We also have the same condition when a foreman produces parts for which the marketing demand is less than his capacity to produce. In all three cases there is a buildup of inventory someplace else in the plant—a spreading of the troops. While the foreman's performance looks good, he increases the overall inventory of the plant but not its throughput. Not exactly what we want to achieve. Is it possible that our work ethic causes our foremen and workers to do the wrong thing?

Maybe we need to consider some cultural changes so that the workers will have an incentive to follow the drumbeat—some way to remove the earmuffs. But even if we were to permit the workers to follow the drummer, are we now beating the drum in a way that they can really follow it?

THE CAUSE OF EXCESS INVENTORIES

X—The slowest soldier—a resource that can barely cope with demand

Y—A faster soldier—a resource with excess capacity

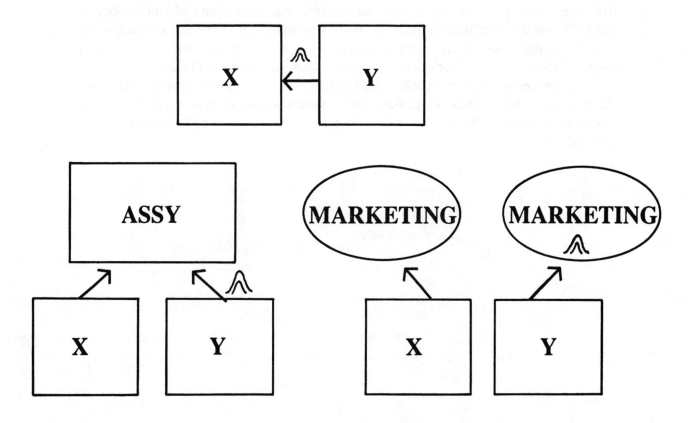

43: CAN WORKERS MARCH TO YOUR DRUMBEAT?

In your plant, does the drum beat according to the constraints of the plant or is it driven by some unrealistic assumptions? For example, do you use a logistical procedure that assumes each resource has infinite capacity—each solider can march as fast as you wish? Not even a single slow soldier exists? If you do, then even if the soldiers try very hard, they cannot always follow the drumbeat. Or does your drumbeat assume that there are predetermined lead times for manufacturing products? Even though the average production time may be three months, when necessary, we all know that we can expedite the completion of any order in just a few days by giving it first priority at each operation.

What is the correct lead time we should use in beating the drum—three months or three days? Maybe the lead time through the plant depends on how we decide to schedule production. If an order follows its normal course it takes three months. If we give it a priority everywhere, it can be completed in a fraction of that time. It looks like we're forced to conclude that lead times cannot be accurately predetermined, but are a function of how we decide to schedule the plant.

Does your drumbeat assume that production will be done in fixed and constant batch sizes even though we are well aware that splitting and overlapping of batches occurs constantly on the shop floor, especially to get shipments out at the end of the month? If your logistical system uses unrealistic assumptions like these, then your drummer has no rhythm. He beats out discordant sounds that no one can follow.

The drummer-sergeant approach looked at first like a very good solution. When we examine more closely how it has been implemented we are forced to admit that it is less than satisfactory. So let's look for another solution, even if at first sight it looks a bit radical.

IN YOUR PLANT . . .

Does the drum beat according to the constraints of the plant or according to some unrealistic assumptions . .

Like:

- **Infinite capacity**
- **Predetermined lead times**
- **Fixed, constant batch sizes**

44:   ROPE THE SOLDIERS TOGETHER LIKE MOUNTAIN CLIMBERS

Let us tie the rows of soldiers together — as if they were mountain climbers. In this way we can limit the spreading (inventory) to the lengths of the ropes. This strange idea is actually being used in plants with great success. It was first tried by Henry Ford when he developed the assembly line. More recently, Taichi Ohno, of Toyota, the father of Just-in-Time, employed it when he developed his highly successful Kanban scheduling system.

Ford linked together production resources by using conveyor belts, physical ropes. Ohno used cards or logistical ropes. Both of these rope systems have proven to be enormously successful and have had far-reaching economic implications. Ford's system worked well for high-volume products manufactured on dedicated equipment. Installation of Ford's assembly lines ushered in an era of mass production and resulted in a huge increase in our standard of living. Ohno's Kanban system extended Ford's idea to repetitively manufactured products produced on non-dedicated equipment. Its installation led to the emergence of Japan as a major economic power. We are seeing clearly the results of Ohno's approach—a substantial increase in the standard of living in Japan and the loss of our dominant position in many industries.

Can we find the secret of the ropes? Will it enable us to win the race?

A TROOP ANALOGY

The invention of Henry Ford
—The assembly line—
Dr. Ohno from Toyota
—The Kanban system—

45: PREDETERMINED BUFFERS MAKE IT WORK

The key to Ford's and Ohno's systems lies not in the conveyor belts or Kanban cards but in the fact that the belts and the cards are mechanisms for establishing a predetermined inventory buffer (rope length) between each two work centers.

On Ford's assembly line the predetermined buffer is the space on the conveyor belt between two operations. In Ohno's approach it is the number of Kanban cards, one for each container of parts, that are predetermined to be used between two operations. The buffer tells the worker at the preceding work center both when to work—and when not to work. When the buffer is full, the preceding worker stops. When the buffer is not full, he works. In these two similar approaches the flow of work is synchronized so that the inventory is quite low compared to our conventional modes of operation.

There is, however, a major drawback to this type of rope system. Any significant disruption at any work center will cause the overall flow to stop and throughput to be lost. These disruptions are very expensive since if they had not occurred, additional products could have been produced for essentially only the cost of the raw materials. This is the reason why extensive attention is given in these rope systems to reducing fluctuations and disruptions in the flow of material. Machines must be much more reliable. Setup time must be reduced and made predictable. Production overloads must be prevented, and so on. To achieve the elimination of these problems is not a trivial task. It requires the same long process that we are familiar with when debugging an assembly, process or transfer line.

Reducing fluctuations under the Kanban system is not less important, and a very long period, sometimes more than ten years, is needed to reduce fluctuation so that the Kanban system can safely be installed. Let us now compare our conventional system and this rope system.

SYNCHRONIZED MANUFACTURING ASSEMBLY LINES AND KANBANS

Predetermined inventory buffers (either limited by space or number of cards) regulate the rate of production for assembly lines and Kanban systems. The instruction given to the worker is

"Stop working when the buffer is filled!"

The work is synchronized, inventory is low . . . but any significant disruption will cause the entire system to stop.

46: THE WESTERN WAY—JUST-IN-CASE

The conventional Western approach can be characterized as a just-in-case system. The drum that dictates when raw materials are going to be released into the plant is held by the excess capacity of the first operation. Remember, when a worker doesn't have any work to do, we find him more material to work on.

The result is considerably higher inventory than in the rope system, but with the advantage that throughput is seemingly protected. Unfortunately, we protect our current throughput at the expense of sacrificing our competitive edge in the market—our future throughput. The reverse is true under the Just-in-Time rope system.

A JUST-IN-CASE SYSTEM

Raw Material ○ ○ ○ ○ ○ ○ ○ ○ Finished Goods

The drum is held by the excess capacity of the gating operations

RESULT:

- **Inventory is high**
- **Current throughput is protected**
- **Furture throughput is in danger**

47: JUST-IN-TIME OR JUST-IN-CASE—THE ROPE OR THE AX?

In the Just-in-Time system, the drum is held by the market demand. The release of raw materials into the plant results from a chain reaction initiated when the final operation supplies material to the marketplace. When products are shipped to a customer, the final operation replaces these goods by withdrawing and processing an equivalent amount of material from the buffer between it and the preceding operation. The use of this material signals the preceding operation to replace the material that has been taken from the buffer. This chain reaction, or pulling of ropes, eventually causes an equivalent amount of raw material to be released into the plant.

This chain reaction is accomplished through some type of signaling device or signboard (Kanban) . The Kanban is often a card that is placed in a standardized container holding a specified number of parts. When a container is taken by the next operation for processing, the card or Kanban is returned to the preceding operation. This Kanban is a signal for the preceding operation to produce another container of parts to replace the one that has been used.

In this approach, inventory is limited by the length of the ropes—predetermined inventory buffers—and is much lower than in the just-in-case approach. Current throughput may be lost whenever a significant disruption occurs, but in the longer run the lower inventory secures future throughput by increasing the competitive edge.

What should we do? Copy the Japanese and adopt the Just-in-Time approach? Unfortunately, we don't have the luxury of the long and arduous period that the installation of such a rope system takes. If we do nothing our heads will be chopped off by our competition. What will we choose? The rope or the ax? Maybe there is a better alternative. Let's go back to our analogy.

A JUST-IN-TIME SYSTEM

Raw Materials ◯━◯━◯━◯━◯━◯━◯ Finished Goods

The drum is held by marketing demands

RESULT:

● Inventory is low
● Current throughput is in danger
● Future throughput is increased

48: A NEW SYSTEM—DBR

Since the weakest soldier dictates the pace, if we allow the first soldier to go faster than the weakest soldier, he will just cause the troop to spread. Why don't we tie a rope directly from the weakest soldier to the first row of soldiers? This is a different approach to synchronizing our troop (manufacturing plant) , so we need a name for it. We'll call it the Drum-Buffer-Rope (DBR) approach.

Let's explore the DBR way to understand its ramifications. The soldiers following the weakest soldier will be able to march faster than him and consequently will always be on his heels (no spreading here) . The first row of soldiers could also march faster than the weakest soldier, but is constrained by the rope to march at the same speed as the weakest soldier. The soldiers between the first row and the weakest soldier are faster than the weakest one and thus will be on the heels of the first row of soldiers. The only gap or spreading will be right in front of the weakest soldier. The size of this gap will be predetermined by the length of the rope that we have chosen.

Let's examine the advantages of this solution. Suppose that one of the soldiers following the weakest soldier drops his gun. Under Ford and Ohno's rope systems, the whole troop will soon be halted. Under the DBR way the weakest soldier's progress will not be affected at all. Some spreading (inventory) will occur because of this disruption, but since the soldiers that follow the weakest soldier are faster (have extra capacity) , they will catch up a little bit later. The spreading will be only temporary and there will be no slowing of the progress of the entire troop (throughput) . We see that the impact of a disturbance on the DBR way is vastly different than on the Just-in-Time approach.

It seems that the DBR way has some advantages, but let's look further. If a soldier preceding the weakest soldier drops his gun, as long as he picks it up before the weakest soldier has closed the gap, there will again be no impact on the troop's rate of movement. The gap (inventory) in front of the weakest soldier serves as a buffer against disruptions from the preceding soldiers (production resources) . By concentrating the inventory just in front of the weakest soldier and causing the first soldier to walk at the weakest soldier's rate, we are gaining the best of both worlds. Inventory is even lower than under Just-in-Time and throughput is even more protected than under just-in-case.

Maybe we have found a much better way to synchronize manufacturing. It looks like we can protect current throughput, enhance future throughput, not endanger operating expense (no more soldiers are needed) and still reduce inventory significantly.

It sounds good, but let's check to see if the DBR way is really applicable in all types of plants. We'll begin by examining a schematic of a simple plant employing this approach.

A TROOP ANALOGY

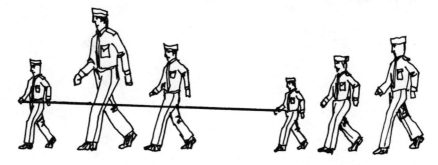

Since the weakest soldier dictates pace

● **To prevent spreading, tie weakest soldier to the front row.**

● **To protect overall pace, provide some slack in the rope.**

49:   DRUMS, BUFFERS AND ROPES

In any plant there are only a few capacity constraint resources (CCR's) —weakest soldiers. The DBR way recognizes that such a constraint will dictate the rate of production of the entire plant. So let's treat the major capacity constraint resource as the drummer. Its production rate will serve as the drumbeat for the entire plant. We will also need to establish an inventory buffer in front of each CCR. This buffer will contain only the inventory needed to keep the CCR busy during the next predetermined time interval (from now on we will refer to such a buffer as the time buffer) . Consequently, this time buffer will protect the throughput of the plant against any disruption that can be overcome within the predetermined time interval.

In order to ensure that inventory will not grow beyond the level dictated by the time buffer, we must limit the rate at which raw material is released into the plant. A rope should be tied from the CCR to the gating (first) operation. In other words, the rate at which the gating operation will be allowed to release material into production will be dictated by the rate at which the CCR is producing.

The concept seems sound, so let's devise a procedure to implement the DBR logistical approach, the drum-buffer-rope system, in a plant. A good logistical system should have the means (plans and schedules) of controlling the flow of material into, through and out of our plants no matter how complicated they may be. It is such a procedure that we need to develop.

SYNCHRONIZED MANUFACTURING
THE DRUM-BUFFER-ROPE WAY

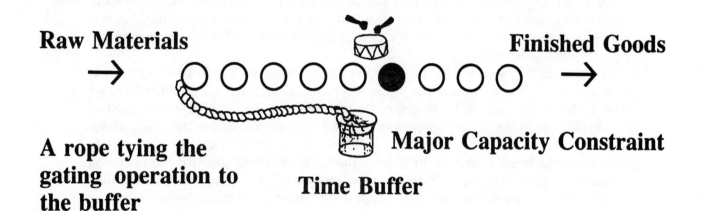

Raw Materials

Finished Goods

A rope tying the gating operation to the buffer

Major Capacity Constraint

Time Buffer

50: DEVISING A DRUM-BUFFER-ROPE SYSTEM

We'll begin by examining a part going through several operations with only one of them being a CCR. This part will eventually be assembled with other parts into a finished product for shipment to several different customers.

Since the two major constraints on the plant are the market demands (the amount of product we can sell) and the capacity of the CCR, it will make sense to base our schedule (logistical flow) on those two constraints. Thus the first step will be to determine the schedule of the CCR by taking into account only its limited capacity and the market demands that it is trying to satisfy. Once the CCR's schedule is established, we need to determine how to schedule all the non-constraining resources. Using the schedule of the CCR, the schedule of the succeeding operations can be derived easily. Once a part is completed at a CCR it can be scheduled to start at the next operation. Each subsequent operation, including assembly, is simply started when the previous operation finishes. In this fashion we can generate schedules for all succeeding operations, including assembly.

The challenge now is to schedule the preceding operations and to protect the CCR from disturbances that might occur at the preceding resources. As we said before, we would like to limit the buffer to a specific time interval. Let's suppose that most of the disruptions at the preceding operations can be overcome within two days. If so, three day's protection in our time buffer looks like it will be sufficient. Now we simply have to schedule backwards in time from the CCR. We will plan for the operation immediately preceding the CCR to complete the needed parts three days before they are scheduled to be run on the CCR. Each of the other preceding operations will be back-scheduled in a similar manner so that the parts are available just-in-time for the following operation.

In this way we can generate a schedule and a time buffer that will satisfy all the requirements laid out in the schematic approach. Any disturbances at the preceding operations that can be overcome within the time buffer will not effect the throughput of the plant. Looks good—throughput is protected, inventory reduced and operating expense is not increased. How do we now schedule other parts fed to the same assembly?

SYNCHRONIZED MANUFACTURING THE DRUM-BUFFER-ROPE WAY

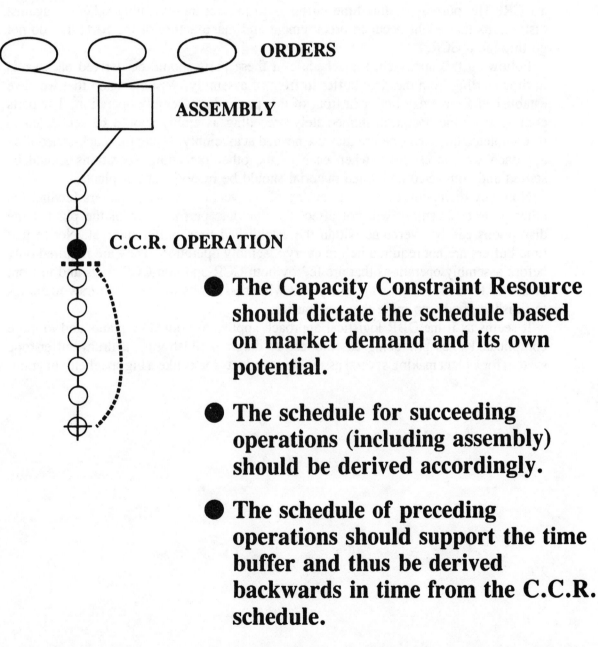

ORDERS

ASSEMBLY

C.C.R. OPERATION

● **The Capacity Constraint Resource should dictate the schedule based on market demand and its own potential.**

● **The schedule for succeeding operations (including assembly) should be derived accordingly.**

● **The schedule of preceding operations should support the time buffer and thus be derived backwards in time from the C.C.R. schedule.**

51: ASSURING HIGH DUE-DATE PERFORMANCE

The procedure laid down so far will protect the throughput of the plant, but meeting customer due dates is also important and needs to be protected as well. In the DBR way, the assembly schedule is dictated by the availability of the scarce parts coming from the CCR. The availability of these scarce parts controls when we can assemble and ship products. Consequently, we should try to prevent the shortage of any other part from disrupting our assembly schedule.

In order to assure that the other parts are available when needed, let's once again build a time buffer, this time in front of the assembly operation requiring a part from a CCR. The purpose of this time buffer is to protect the assembly schedule against disruptions that might occur in procurement and manufacture of the parts that do not go through a CCR.

Following this approach, the schedule of these parts should be derived backwards in time starting from the time buffer in front of assembly. Assume again that we have established a three-day buffer in front of this particular assembly operation. The parts coming from the operation immediately preceding assembly should be scheduled to be completed three days before they are needed at assembly. Using this back-scheduling approach we can establish when each of the other preceding operations should be started and completed and when material should be received at our plants.

Now any disruption that occurs at any of the vendors or work centers feeding the other parts to assembly will not affect the due-date performance of the plant if the disruptions can be overcome within the established time buffer interval. Notice that time buffers are not required before every assembly operation. They are required only before assembly operations that are fed by both CCR and non-CCR parts and in front of the CCR itself. In this way, every part will cross, in its journey from raw materials to finished goods, no more than one buffer.

It seems as if the DBR logistical approach applies to both flow plants and to more complicated ones producing assemblies. A diagram illustrating a drum-buffer-rope system for a plant making several assembled products looks like a big spaghetti diagram.

SYNCHRONIZED MANUFACTURING
THE DRUM-BUFFER-ROPE WAY

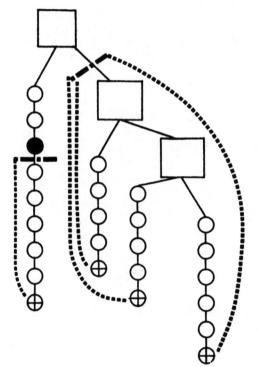

- **All other operation schedules must support the assembly schedule.**

- **To avoid harm due to disruptions, they should support a time buffer in front of any assembly that uses a C.C.R. part.**

- **Inventory is low, but nevertheless any disruption that can be overcome within the buffer time will not affect the throughput of the plant.**

52: UNIVERSAL APPLICATION

In any plant, no matter how large or complex, there are only a limited number of CCR's. Every CCR can be protected by a time buffer and so can the assemblies fed by them. Ropes can be tied from each buffer to the gating operations and any fork points. It looks as if there is no limit to the application of a drum-buffer-rope system.

The concept of the DBR logistical system is quite clear, but the complexity of this diagram illustrates why we will need the aid of a computerized system. Even though the calculations are quite straightforward, to perform them manually in almost every plant is very time consuming and requires heavenly patience.

In implementing such a procedure, the first question that jumps into our mind is how we can quickly identify which of the production resources are CCR's.

SYNCHRONIZED MANUFACTURING

THE DRUM-BUFFER-ROPE WAY

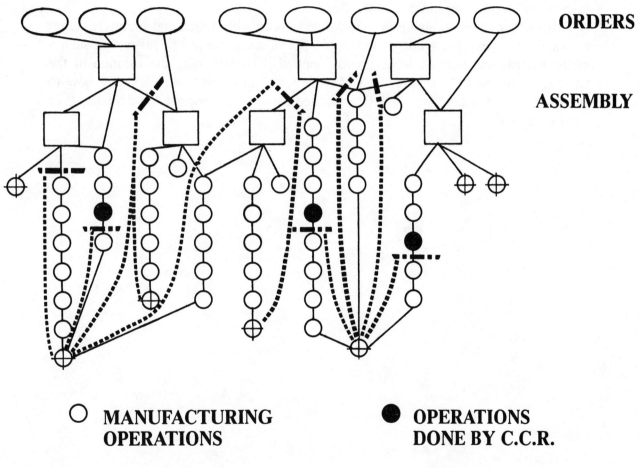

ORDERS

ASSEMBLY

○ MANUFACTURING OPERATIONS   ● OPERATIONS DONE BY C.C.R.

▪▬▪ TIME BUFFERS   .... ROPES

IN ANY PLANT THERE ARE VERY FEW CAPACITY CONSTRAINT RESOURCES.

53: LOCATING THE CONSTRAINTS

At first glance, locating the CCR's seems to be a formidable and possibly unending task. True, in some plants there is a good understanding of which operations are CCR's. In other types of plants the CCR's are referred to as floating bottlenecks that wander all over the plant. In still other types of plants, the locations are not at all clear and it appears that a tremendous amount of time and research would be needed to locate them.

While our task initially appears to be a mammoth one, there is a solution. The key is in recognizing that a constraint of the entire plant (e. g. a CCR) must manifest itself in every aspect of the business. Building on this insight, we can devise a straightforward approach that enables us to take surprisingly little time to zoom from the various impacts of a constraint directly to its location.

This method, even though it is well-defined, thoroughly tested and routinely taught to others is beyond the scope of this book. So let's assume at this stage that such a method exists and that we have already applied it to determine the location of the CCR's. Once the CCR's have been identified, the next question is exactly how to schedule them in accordance with their limited capacity and the market demands they need to satisfy.

SYNCHRONIZED MANUFACTURING

LOCATING THE CONSTRAINTS

First step toward synchronized manufacturing is to identify the constraints.

A capacity constraint manifests itself in all of the major business issues.

An analysis of the major business issues can be used to identify the capacity constraint resources (CCR's).

54:   HOW TO BEAT THE DRUM

A CCR limits the throughput of the plant and controls due-date performance. We have to ensure, on the one hand, that the CCR is not scheduled to produce more than it's capacity and on the other hand not to waste any of its capacity by allowing any slack in its schedule. Finally, we have to sequence production at the CCR in a manner that will result in good due-date performance.

We can accomplish these goals by employing a method that is used by almost every foreman. First, simply schedule forward in time from the present. Decide what product to schedule first, how many are needed and how long it will take to produce them. Then repeat the procedure. When the available capacity for the first day is used up, begin scheduling the second day, and so on. The only remaining problem is how to choose the sequence in which the various products are to be done by the CCR. A good first rough cut sequence is given by the customer due dates of the required products. We probably would like to work first on a product needed by a customer two days from now before working on a product needed next week.

Sequencing production at the CCR based on the customer due date is a sound approach, but there are four cases that might cause us to modify these sequencing decisions.

SYNCHRONIZED MANUFACTURING BEATING THE DRUM

Ensure maximum throughput through forward scheduling of the C.C.R.'s.

Due dates give us the first, rough sequence, but the sequence must be modified under any one of four conditions . . .

55: FOUR CONDITIONS THAT COMPLICATE SCHEDULING

The first case occurs when lead time from the CCR operation to the completion of the product is greatly different for different products. We might have a Product A that, once it has been completed by the CCR, requires only one day of additional work before it can be shipped. Product B may require an entire week at the operations following the CCR before it can be shipped. When these circumstances exist, it may make sense to modify the CCR customer due-date sequence at the CCR so that we work on Product B which is due for shipment next week before working on Product A even though it is due to be shipped this week.

A second condition that may cause us to deviate from the customer due-date sequence arises whenever one CCR is feeding another CCR. In such a case, by obeying the market due-date sequence at the first CCR we may starve the second CCR. We don't have to lose time on all CCR's in order to lose throughput of the entire plant. To lose time on just one of them is enough. Remember the value of this lost time. If it had not been lost, we could have shipped additional products for essentially the raw material costs.

A third common situation occurs when the process on a CCR also involves setup—effort and time required for the resource to be changed from producing one product to another. In such an event, we will sometimes prefer to make a single production run to satisfy the market demands of a particular product for several days, saving several setups, rather than follow the exact customer due-date sequence. In this way we can use more of the scarce CCR capacity for actual production and less for setting up.

There is a fourth common situation that is less recognized but no less important. It occurs whenever a CCR is producing more than one part for the same product. In this case, the customer due date will not guide us at all in choosing the sequence, since all the parts have the same due date. Nevertheless, the resulting performance of the plant can be greatly influenced by the sequence we choose.

The task of choosing a good sequence in each of these four cases is more complicated than setting the sequence based solely on customer due date. However, good rules can be established and incorporated into a computerized system. But we must stress that the real importance lies more in the overall application of the drum-buffer-rope method than the precise way that the drum is beaten.

The technical details of constructing such as a system can be, and have been, overcome. The real difficulties that can prevent a company from fully and quickly capitalizing on the drum-buffer-rope approach do not lie in the technical details. They lie in the fact that the drum-buffer-rope method is in direct conflict with some deeply rooted behavior patterns.

SYNCHRONIZED MANUFACTURING

BEATING THE DRUM

Complicating conditions:

- Different lead times from capacity constraint resources to due dates

- One capacity constraint resource feeding another one

- Set up on a capacity constraint resource

- A capacity constraint resource feeding more than one part to the same product

56: DBR BUFFERS CLASH WITH OUR CULTURE

We have agreed that it seems logical to concentrate all the inventory protection just before the crucial operations and not to use inventory to protect every place where a disruption can occur. While this seems logical, it is contrary to the behavior of almost every foreman. Foremen are accustomed to buffering themselves with floats of inventory so that they can respond to any urgent demand from succeeding operations, which they know all too well will occur at the worst possible time.

A very persuasive education must be given to the foreman before he will abandon this long-held pack rat mentality. Remember we are asking him to give up his visible protection, one that he controls, in return for a promise that somewhere, maybe not even in his department, inventory is kept to protect the entire plant. We are not dealing here with a change in the foreman's personal culture, but a culture controlled by how management measures a foreman's performance.

Our buffer only-at-critical operations concept clashes not only with a foreman's culture, it clashes even more strongly with the culture of upper management. We have just agreed that inventory of the right parts, in the right quantities, at the right time, in front of the right operations, gives very good protection. We have even described a procedure to implement this concept. We have also agreed that because of the frantic race for a competitive edge that work-in-process inventory anywhere else is destructive.

These two ideas, while logically compelling, are very much at odds with current management thinking about inventory. Managements need to reanalyze and reassess their reasons for holding inventory. The perceived reasons may be at odds with the financial ramification of the competitive edge analysis outlined previously. A deep soul-searching is needed to overcome the accepted practices of many generations.

The buffer concept flies in the face of our ingrained culture, but its implications pale in light of the impact of the rope concept.

SYNCHRONIZED MANUFACTURING

LOCATING THE TIME BUFFERS

● Concentrate protection not at the origin of a disturbance, but before critical operations

● Inventory of the right parts in the right quantities at the right times in front of the right operations gives high protection

● Inventory anywhere else is destructive

57: DBR ROPES REQUIRE A CHANGE IN MANAGEMENTS BEHAVIOR

We can readily accept the logic that requires us to release and process materials according to the schedule determined by the plant constraints (the rope concept) . Once we do, we have to face the fact that this conclusion means that under no circumstances should we release materials just to supply work to workers. This is probably the most difficult behavior pattern that has to be overcome.

The Japanese have an advantage, a lead in the competitive edge race, because they went through this cultural shock a decade ago. Imagine an expensive machine run by a highly paid worker with some expensive, half-processed parts sitting in front of it. These parts are going to be needed to assemble customer orders in just four hours. Nevertheless, the worker is not running the machine. He is standing idle.

What will be your response to such a situation? Once you have recovered from your heart attack you probably will deal very severely with the worker and his foreman. The Japanese response in Just-In-Time plants is quite different. Under a Kanban system (the JIT scheduling system) , as long as this worker does not have a Kanban card, this is precisely what he is supposed.to do—not produce parts. This difference in behavior is not because of a difference in the culture of countries or workers but is due to a drastically different culture of management.

The Japanese have recognized and proven the tremendous benefits of such a management cultural change. We must now make the same behavioral change or withdraw from the race. It is management's task to create the cultural change needed for the acceptance of these concepts. The procedure for creating the necessary supporting schedules and simulating (what ifs) the flow of material and use of resources can be readily accomplished through computer software.

The drum-buffer-rope concepts are straightforward, readily understood and to a degree can be capitalized on without the use of a software system. The need for the assistance of software increases with the amount of data, changes (e. g. forecast variations) and what ifs that must be dealt with. It may become a necessity as the number of CCR's increases and the four complicating conditions become more prevalent. It is probably essential if a company wishes to establish a focused process of ongoing improvement.

SYNCHRONIZED MANUFACTURING ROPES

 Release and process material according to the schedule determined by the plant constraints

 Do not release material in order to supply work to workers

58: DBR AND A PROCESS OF ONGOING, FOCUSED IMPROVEMENT

Installing a drum-buffer-rope system can get a company back into the competitive edge race. In fact the results of such installations and the relatively short time required to achieve outstanding benefits are truly impressive. However, a drum-buffer-rope system will not enable a company to stay in or lead the race for long.

We must not look for just an improvement in our performance, no matter how significant. We must find a way to establish an ongoing, never ending process of improvement. We know that we need to improve in our plants. Unfortunately there are an almost unlimited number of improvements possible. We know that we can't do everything at once, so where do we start? What specific improvements will move us closest to our goal? It would be even better if we had a procedure that could be used routinely to determine which improvements are the most important at any point in time. There is such a process of ongoing, focused improvement.

We have seen the importance of the capacity constraints to throughput and inventory and why they need to be buffered against the many daily disruptions that occur in a plant. A careful observation of these buffers can tell us a great deal about the inevitable fluctuations in our plant and its marketplace. Understanding how to properly manage the inventory buffers can both improve our immediate competitive edge position (since most of our inventory is now in the buffers) and serve to pinpoint the improvements most needed to further enhance it.

While this process of ongoing improvement can be used to focus and synchronize *almost all* management efforts in a manufacturing company, we will illustrate here only an example of how it can be used to focus process improvements.

The following illustrations demonstrate how to manage the buffers and to use them as a crystal ball to locate and quantify the importance of the disruptions in a plant. Correcting those highlighted disruptions, continual usage of the drum-buffer-rope approach to synchronize flow and manage the buffers will enable us to establish an ongoing, focused process of improvement—a productivity flywheel.

In order to better understand how, let's first look in more detail at a time buffer.

SYNCHRONIZED MANUFACTURING THE DRUM-BUFFER-ROPE WAY

In the midst of a competitive edge race we should not look for an improvement, we should look to implement a process of

on-going improvement.

59:   UNDERSTANDING TIME BUFFERS

Suppose that the schedule has been set for a CCR for an entire week. This schedule calls for the processing of various parts in various quantities throughout the days of the week. The same part may appear more than once on this dispatch list since the sequence is set by customer due dates and modified whenever any of the four complicating conditions exist.

If we stick to our example of choosing a time buffer of three days, on Monday morning we expect to find in front of the CCR all the parts that the CCR is scheduled to do on Monday, Tuesday and Wednesday. We do not want to find in front of the CCR any other parts. Accumulating more parts there will not add significantly to our protection and it will reduce our competitive edge in the market.

We have chosen to depict the time buffer as a rectangle. The vertical axis represents the number of hours that a particular part will require of the CCR. The horizontal axis measures when (e. g. what day) these parts are scheduled to be processed by the CCR.

At any point in time, we have a fixed predetermined time buffer, but the content of the time buffer, as we shall see, is continually changing.

SYNCHRONIZED MANUFACTURING THE TIME BUFFERS

A schedule of CCR

DAY	PART	QU.	HOURS
MON.	A	25	5
	B	5	3
TUES.	B	5	3
	C	5	5
WED.	C	2	2
	D	2	6
THURS.	D	1	3
	A	25	5
FRI.	C	2	2
	B	10	6

Choosing a buffer of three days. The planned buffer content on Monday morning.

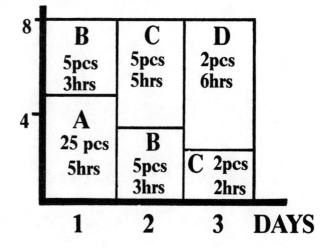

HOURS OF WORK AVAILABLE TO THE CCR

No other part should be in front of the CCR.

60: BUFFER CONTENT—CONSTANTLY CHANGING

The content of our buffer on Tuesday morning should be different. We now expect to find only the parts that the schedule of the CCR calls for on Tuesday, Wednesday and Thursday. The parts scheduled for Monday should have already been completed and the parts scheduled for processing by the CCR on Friday should not have arrived yet. This concept of revolving inventory in the buffer is vastly different from the usual understanding of safety stock as a constant inventory level for each part.

We have chosen to portray the buffer content in the form of a rectangle. By presenting it in this way, we can see the quantity of parts needed, the sequence in which they are going to be consumed and the amount of hours of work of the CCR that they are protecting. This approach enables us to analyze the actual and planned content of the buffer and to determine actions that will improve both our immediate and longer term competitive edge.

SYNCHRONIZED MANUFACTURING

THE TIME BUFFERS

A schedule of CCR

DAY	PART	QU.	HOURS
MON.	A	25	5
	B	5	3
TUES.	B	5	3
	C	5	5
WED.	C	2	2
	D	2	6
THURS.	D	1	3
	A	25	5
FRI.	C	2	2
	B	10	6

The planned buffer content on Tuesday morning.

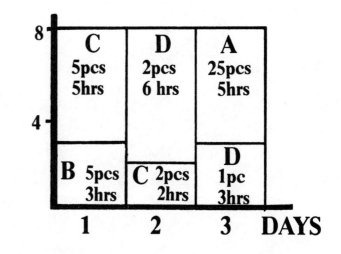

HOURS OF WORK AVAILABLE TO THE CCR

The buffer content is changing from one day to the other in accordance with the CCR schedule.

61: ACTUAL BUFFERS SHOULD DIFFER FROM PLANNED BUFFERS

How can an analysis of the time buffer point the way to actions that immediately improve our competitive edge? We know that one purpose of the buffers is to protect the throughput and due-date performance of the plant against the impact of disruptions. If disruptions occur, we should expect to find that the actual content of the buffer is smaller than we planned. If the buffer is always full, it is a sure sign that there are no disruptions significant enough to affect the planned material flow. Consequently, a buffer is not needed and this inventory can be eliminated without damage to throughput or operating expense. In fact, by eliminating the buffer we will reduce operating expense.

If the actual buffer in front of a critical operation should not be the same as the planned buffer, what should it look like? The desired planned and actual buffer pattern is illustrated in the facing example. The material planned to be in the first third of the time buffer, the material that is consumed first by the CCR, should always be present. On the other hand, we should expect to find that most of the material planned for the last third of the buffer is missing. The actual versus planned contents of the middle third of the buffer should lie somewhere in between these two extremes. This buffer profile should protect our critical operations from all but the most extreme fluctuations.

Let's see what actions we can take to improve our competitive edge immediately if the actual content of the buffer deviates from this pattern.

SYNCHRONIZED MANUFACTURING TIME BUFFERS

The time buffer contains most of the inventory and should protect the plant against disruptions

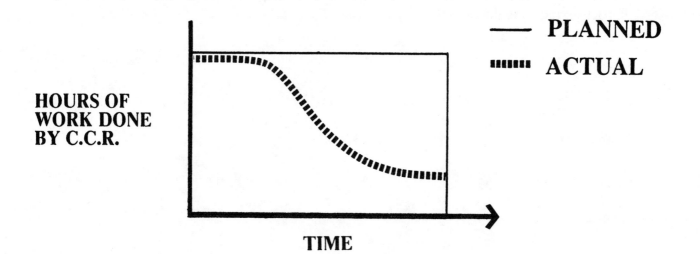

The actual buffer must be smaller than planned if disruptions exist. Otherwise, there is no need for a buffer at all

62: MANAGING THE TIME BUFFERS

If the pattern of the actual buffer stretches beyond the planned buffer, as in Case 1, then it is a clear indication that material is being produced earlier than called for at preceding operations. This pattern suggests that material is being released prematurely to the first operation. Management probably has not totally implemented the cultural change required for a drum-buffer-rope system. More education and discipline is probably needed at the gating operation.

If the buffer is almost full as in Case 2, we have a clear indication that the planned buffer is too large. We are paying too high a premium for insurance. We should cut the size of the planned buffer to the point where only the first third of the buffer is totally filled. In Case 3, the totally filled portion is less than the first third of the buffer, indicating that the buffer is too small and we run the risk of starving the CCR and losing throughput. The planned buffer needs to be immediately increased until the first third is completely full.

We can see why it is important to have the appropriate amount of emptiness in the buffer and where it should be located, but we should also be taking action to eliminate vacancies or holes in the buffer. If we can prevent these holes from occurring then we can further reduce the buffer size and increase our competitive edge. How can we get an indication where, with the minimum amount of effort, we can have the maximum impact on reducing the buffer?

SYNCHRONIZED MANUFACTURING BUFFER MANAGEMENT

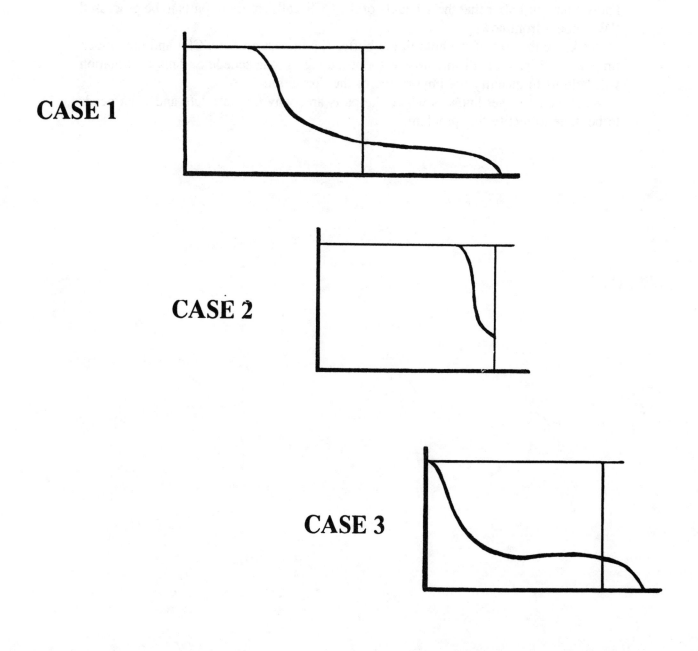

CASE 1

CASE 2

CASE 3

63: HOLES IN THE BUFFERS

A comparison of the planned and actual buffers will reveal the parts that are missing from the buffer that should be there. These parts, or holes, in the buffer are caused by disruptions in the flow of material at preceding operations or from our vendors.

At this point, we do not know where this material is or why it is late to the buffer. We do know that it must still be at one of the preceding operations (or a vendor) . Our illustration shows that a certain quantity of part A that was planned to be in the buffer has not yet arrived, creating a hole in the buffer. These missing parts will require "Y" hours of the CCR's capacity when they do arrive and are processed. We also know from our buffer that the schedule of the CCR calls for these parts to be processed "W" hours from now.

We know the size of the hole in the buffer (its impact on the CCR) and how much time we still have to fill this hole without damaging our schedule. This information will help us to quantify the importance of the disruption.

What we don't yet know is where the parts are, why they are late and what needs to be done to rectify this problem.

SYNCHRONIZED MANUFACTURING

FOCUSING IMPROVEMENTS

Discrepancy between planned and actual buffers reveals the disruptions to material flow

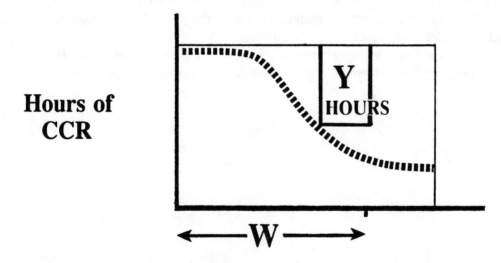

Hours of CCR

A hole representing *Y hours* of *Part A* inventory scheduled to be worked on in *W hours* are missing.

This information can be used to quantify the disruption.

64: CALCULATING A DISRUPTION FACTOR

We can determine the location of the missing parts by checking our inventory control system or by simply going and looking. Once we have determined the location of these parts, we have a very good indication of which work center or vendor caused the disruption in the flow. The disruptive source is *most likely* the work center or vendor that the part is currently sitting in front of.

Now that we know the location of the material, we can devise a procedure to quantify the importance of this disruption relative to other disruptions causing holes in this and other buffers. Only three parameters are needed and we already know two of them. The first is "Y, " the number of hours that the CCR should spend processing these parts. This parameter reflects the magnitude of the damage that will be caused if the material will not arrive at the buffer on time. The second is the protection time "W" that is still left until the CCR will be impacted by the absence of this material. The third one is "P, " the amount of processing time required to complete the parts so they can be processed by the CCR.

Using this information we can calculate a single number, or disruption factor for each hole in the buffer and assign it to the disruptive work center. The larger the disruption factor, the more important it is to eliminate the source of the disruption. Bear in mind that in the case that the material is not in the plant, this disruption factor corresponds to a particular vendor.

We now know the relative importance of all the disruptions in our plant. How do we take advantage of this information to increase our competitive edge?

SYNCHRONIZED MANUFACTURING
FOCUSING IMPROVEMENTS

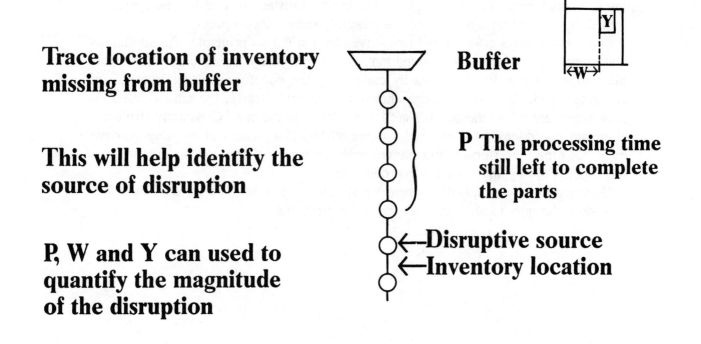

Trace location of inventory missing from buffer

This will help identify the source of disruption

P, W and Y can used to quantify the magnitude of the disruption

Buffer

P The processing time still left to complete the parts

←**Disruptive source**
←**Inventory location**

65: THE PARETO PRINCIPLE

We can repeat these calculations for every hole in every buffer in our plant. If we sum these disruption factors for each source we can arrive at a "disruption factor" for each resource and vendor. The size of the disruption factor tells us the importance of the source in disrupting the flow of materials. We now know not just the relative importance of each disruption, but also the relative importance of each disruption source.

These work center/vendor disruption factors become our priority list for pinpointing where we should concentrate our productivity improvement efforts. Of course, we should deal first with the work center/vendor that has the largest disruption factor. Even if it is difficult to analyze and correct those disruptions, we certainly should not be distracted and correct an easy problem at a work center further down the list. The only result of correcting such a disruption will be the satisfaction that we are correcting something, but it will not have any meaningful bottom line impact.

Our improvement efforts should be driven by the Pareto principle. Pareto claimed that there were always a few important things and many trivial ones. The facing illustration portrays Pareto's idea by contrasting the benefits resulting from an improvement with the cost of making that improvement. Clearly, the most desired improvements are where the benefits are large relative to the cost. Constantly striving to eliminate disruptions that cause holes in the buffers is a process of ongoing improvement. Gearing our efforts to the sources with the largest disruption factors is part of this process of ongoing, focused improvement.

Once we locate and quantify where we should concentrate, we have a whole host of good techniques to analyze and correct the problems.

SYNCHRONIZED MANUFACTURING

FOCUSING IMPROVEMENTS

Repeating the same process for every hole in every buffer and summing the magnitude of the disruption for each work center will give us a disruption factor for each work center in the plant

These disruption factors are our priority list for focusing our productivity improvement efforts.

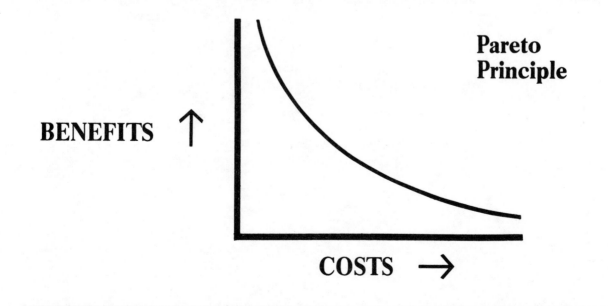

66: MAKING SENSE OF THE ALPHABET SOUP

Our disruption factors tell us where to concentrate and how important it is to make the improvement. They do not tell us what caused the disruption. We must analyze the source to determine the major cause of the largest disruption factors.

A work center might be disrupting the flow because of frequent machine breakdowns. Here is where our preventative maintenance efforts should be focused. In the case of an old, unreliable machine, maybe a new one should be acquired or the largest cause of the disruption might instead be a quality problem. Dr. Deming, Dr. Juran and others have provided us with a whole host of very powerful techniques on how to isolate and resolve quality problems.

It might also be that the disruption is caused by a long and unreliable setup. Here is where we should use the detailed setup reduction techniques developed by the Japanese. Or it could be that the disruption was caused by a foreman trying to make his department look efficient. He might be running bigger batches than required, in order to save setups, but as a result causing a disruption in the flow of needed material. We might deal with this problem by using the "old Missouri mule technique."

These illustrations are examples of how this process of ongoing improvement can focus our alphabet soup of available improvement techniques into a powerful, coherent force. Each of the improvement techniques can be either extremely beneficial (if it has a global impact) or a waste of money (where it has only a local impact). Since inventory is closely linked to the six competitive edge elements, we can use the time buffers to pinpoint the most critical areas for improvement. We should then apply the appropriate technique, and continually repeat this process at the next most important point. We should not apply any or all of these techniques everywhere.

There are a number of other causes of disruptions, and equally effective techniques available to eliminate them. Correcting the problem of the work center (or the vendor) appearing highest on the list will have the greatest impact on filling the most important holes in the buffer, enabling us to reduce the buffer size and repeat the process. As the buffers are reduced, the impact is sure to come.

SYNCHRONIZED MANUFACTURING

FOCUSING IMPROVEMENTS

The work center with the highest disruption factor must be analyzed for causes:

- **Maintenance**
- **Quality**
- **Long unreliable setups**
- **Other**

Once improvements occur, the major holes will disappear and the time buffers can be reduced.

67: REDUCING DISRUPTIONS TO GAIN A COMPETITIVE EDGE

Focused application of the right productivity improvement technique reduces disruptions and eliminates the most important holes in our buffers. As the buffers are decreased, since they contain the majority of the work-in-process inventory, the competitive edge of the plant is increased. Lead times, operating expense and inventory investment will decrease while quality, due-date performance and the speed of introducing improved products will increase.

The market will respond with increasing demand that will lead to a throughput increase. This additional throughput should be very profitable since a commensurate increase in operating expense and inventory is not required. Net profit, return on investment and cash flow will increase simultaneously. We will be moving in the direction of our goal.

However, the elimination of the most important sources of disruption and the increased volume will change our plant and how and where we should focus our efforts.

SYNCHRONIZED MANUFACTURING FOCUSING IMPROVEMENTS

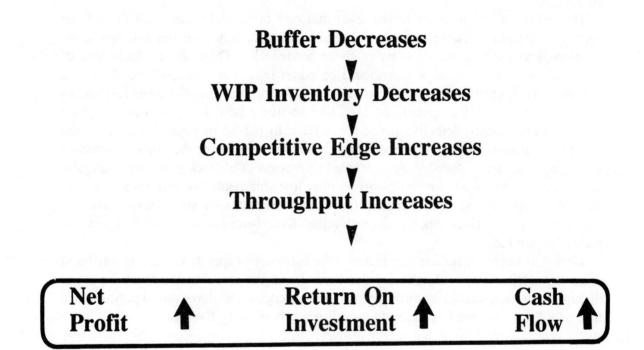

Buffer Decreases

▼

WIP Inventory Decreases

▼

Competitive Edge Increases

▼

Throughput Increases

▼

| Net Profit ↑ | Return On Investment ↑ | Cash Flow ↑ |

68: DEALING WITH BOTTLENECKS

The throughput increase will reduce the excess capacity in the plant, causing the time available to recover from disruptions to decrease. We have been protecting our plant against disruptions with both our inventory buffers and the excess capacity of our stronger soldiers. The stronger soldiers now will have less capacity to catch up quickly if they drop their guns. Now disruptions might cause the slowest soldier (CCR) to stop from time to time (a loss of throughput) . We now need to increase the buffers we have worked so diligently to reduce. Plant personnel need to constantly work on reducing the buffers by eliminating the most important sources of disruption no matter how much the buffers are flexed to account for changing market demands and plant conditions.

Throughput might increase to the level that real bottlenecks that limit throughput appear in the plant. There is not yet a need to immediately rush out and buy more equipment to increase the capacity of these bottlenecks. There are a whole host of quicker, less expensive steps that should be taken first. For example, we should be certain that a bottleneck is always manned, even during lunch hours, other rest breaks and shift changes. Care needs to be exercised so that a bottleneck does not work on parts that are already defective (even if we have to put an inspector in front of the bottleneck) because wasted bottleneck time is lost throughput for the plant. Operations following a bottleneck need to be instructed to process bottleneck parts very carefully because every damaged part represents another lost shipment. We can squeeze a substantial amount of additional capacity from our bottlenecks by such inexpensive and effective methods. Only when these techniques have been exhausted should new capacity be purchased.

The effort to reduce buffers and increase the bottleneck capacity on an ongoing basis is a very profitable one. By shifting our focus from just reducing the most important disruptions to also increasing throughput at the bottlenecks, we have raised performance to a new level. We are beginning to establish a productivity flywheel.

SYNCHRONIZED MANUFACTURING
FOCUSING IMPROVEMENTS

Throughput Increases

Less excess capacity to cope with disruptions

Bottlenecks that limit increased production

Buffer Increase

Inexpensive alternatives to buying more machines

The need to continue to reduce the Buffers

Capacity increase

Net Profit ↑ **Return On Investment** ↑ **Cash Flow** ↑

69: THE PRODUCTIVITY FLYWHEEL

The first step in establishing such a productivity flywheel is to implement synchronized manufacturing using the drum-rope-buffer approach. Then we need to manage the inventory buffers and to focus our process improvement efforts. Finally, Just-in-Time techniques, new technology and good management practices should be brought to bear where they will have the greatest impact. The result will be a continuous increase in net profit, return on investment and cash flow.

Establishing an ongoing, focused improvement process requires that we understand the location of the real constraints of our plants. Once we do, we should zoom in on these constraints applying all our efforts to break them. When a constraint has been removed, we have a new plant and our efforts should now be spent in other areas. We need to find where the new constraints are and attack them with the same fierceness. Remember, even if the constraints are external to the plant (e. g. we have plenty of capacity but not enough market demand) , it is still within our power to affect them. Driving work-in-process inventory down will increase our competitive edge and cause our market demand to increase.

This continual effort to find the current constraints, break them, find the next constraints, break them and so on is an extremely powerful process of ongoing, focused improvement. It is a way for Western industry not only to get back into the race but also to leapfrog over our competition.

We should use this process of ongoing improvement to drive the productivity flywheel at an ever-increasing speed.

BUT REMEMBER. . .

THE COMPETITIVE EDGE RACE PRODUCTIVITY FLYWHEEL

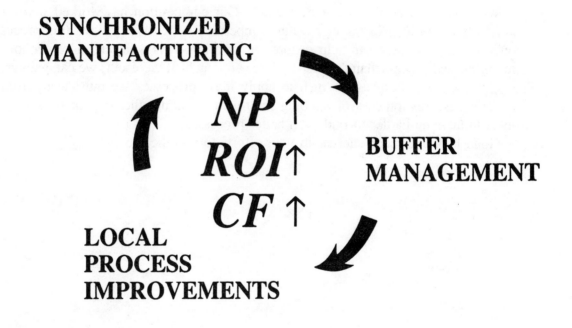

SYNCHRONIZED
MANUFACTURING

NP ↑
ROI ↑
CF ↑

BUFFER
MANAGEMENT

LOCAL
PROCESS
IMPROVEMENTS

JIT
TECHNOLOGY
MANAGEMENT

70: THERE IS NO FINISH LINE

The race for a competitive edge is akin to man's progress—it should be ongoing and without end. We can always do better. When we gain and appply a better understanding of how our manufacturing world works, many benefit. Progress in manufacturing and a rising standard of living have marched hand in hand since the start of the industrial revolution.

What characterizes our world today is the almost brutal intensity of the race and the fact that we are clearly losing it. The implications of this trend are very disturbing to contemplate. Our positions as world powers and our standards of living are clearly at risk. To reverse these trends we need to establish in our organizations an ongoing focused process of improvement. We need to disregard forever the myriad excuses that have prevented us from facing the real problem.

We have been beaten at our own game. Our competition has worked *smarter* not *harder* than us to gain their growing competitive edge. We believe this process of ongoing improvement can help restore our position. It is a faster, more economical, more focused process than the Just-In-Time approach. If we use it, we can gain ground in this race. Even so, as we rush to apply these processes we must learn from our experiences.This process of ongoing improvement is not the only or best way. We must think even harder to find even better processes.

Good luck and much success in your efforts to win the race.

THERE IS NO FINISH LINE!

Appendix A

A Process of
Ongoing Improvement

A PROCESS OF ONGOING IMPROVEMENT

THE MARKETPLACE today is more crowded, faster-changing and more fiercely competitive than at any time in history.

Industrial manufacturing is witnessing an intensification of the race for market-dominance: the life-cycles of products are shortening; zero-defects is becoming the goal of quality; new machine technology is being introduced each year and systems to control production replace each other at an unprecedented rate.

What was once relatively gradual change has in recent years turned into a race of exponentially increasing intensity. Those unable *to continually improve* are falling behind, since success in this environment requires more than a one-time improvement.

Each improvement does of course buy some precious time, but the race in the market continues relentlessly; the slope of the curve grows steeper and the time bought by any one improvement becomes shorter.

Clearly, something far greater than a few sporadic improvements is now needed. Indeed, the only way to secure and improve one's competitive position today is by instituting a process of ongoing improvement.

In the absence of such a process, the many improvements needed are certain to be sporadic and fragmented wasting a great deal of energy, time and resources.

What is required is a process which will, at any moment, identify clearly the area where an improvement will yield the maximum global impact.

This process must enable an organization to achieve the maximum gain from such improvements, while simultaneously helping it to identify the area where the next improvement is needed and to quantify the impact.

Since experience of how to implement such a process is both rare and badly needed we have described below our understanding of the root cause of the inherent resistance to such a process and some of ways we have developed for breaking down this resistance.

NOBODY would disagree that a process capable of generating an evolving, ongoing improvement would be beneficial, but anyone who has tried to introduce any new process to an organization knows all too well the multitude of obstacles encountered.

Experience shows that when these obstacles are closely examined, most will be found rooted in the resistance of the people affected.

Although this resistance may take different forms in various environments, the fact remains that in order to achieve the goal of introducing a process of ongoing improvement, one has to accept and deal with the root cause of this reaction.

There is in fact nothing more difficult for any organization than change—any change. Each improvement is by definition a change, although in the right direction, and each will predictably be met with resistance, despite its beneficial potential.

As for a *process* of improvement, it is by its very nature a process of continual change. The degree of resistance facing it may therefore be quite significant, although of course not all of it conscious. Resistance may come from any tier of the corporate structure, for a change can be as unwelcome in the boardroom as on the factory floor.

If, however, one accepts the existence of a fierce race to survive and flourish in the market, and that one must have a competitive edge, then there is no alternative to instituting such a process of continuing improvement.

Yet our deeply rooted, almost instinctive tendency to reject change makes the introduction of such a process extremely difficult, if not impossible.

Change is opposed, from wherever it may come, not because the change itself was ill-conceived, but simply because it is a change.

While one can try to crush opposition to change, this approach is a trying and time-consuming effort even when successful. To yield to resistance means, however, to give up the only effective, long-lasting remedy to the problem; hence the initial task is to change people's attitude towards change, to neutralize opposition.

How can that be achieved?

Understanding Attitudes Towards Change

WE NEED first of all to try to understand the very different attitudes people have towards improvements, as contrasted with their response to change.

Although both are by definition changes, "improvement", unlike change, carries a positive connotation. Is the key simply need to get others to understand the beneficial nature of the change which we propose?

Let us look at our personal experience. How many times have we tried to explain an innovation to others, whether they are our superiors, subordinates or peers, and felt that somehow the message simply did not get through? We may even have provided flawlessly logical arguments, crystal-clear explanations and eye-opening examples, but still our listeners have remained unconvinced and stubbornly sceptical about the value of what we proposed.

We may often have been left with the feeling that, although they heard us, they didn't really listen. Their energy seemed directed not at evaluating our proposal, but at finding out why it would not work. If we succeeded at all in conveying our message and, perhaps in having it embraced by all, then we managed to do so only thanks to great effort and perseverance.

Clearly, such a method of introducing an improvement is utterly inappropriate when trying to gain acceptance of a process of ongoing improvement.

If we analyze our experience of introducing improvements, we are led inexorably to the conclusion that the resistance we encounter derives more from emotion than logic. Our proposal was perceived more as a change and less as an improvement and, as discussed before, change invariably raises emotional resistance at every level.

In fact, emotions are rarely involved only at the receiving end. Our own emotions, not just our logic, probably helped us to persist and, finally succeed in implementing our improvement.

If we are the champion of an idea, we tend to identify strongly with it, often so much so that others regard it as our "baby." The process of introducing improvements is partly an emotional struggle, with the emotions involved in resisting change being finally overcome only by the stronger emotions of the champion of change.

Our subject, however, is less the emotional nature of human beings than how to come to terms with, and even possibly use, this emotional tendency so deeply ingrained in all of us.

If it were possible for everyone in an organization to convince themselves of the need to adopt a process of ongoing improvement, then each individual would personally acquire an "ownership" of that idea. Then each person's emotional energy would be directed towards embracing this process, rather than rejecting it.

But how can one hope to achieve such a sense of universal, yet individual ownership—and have it occur simultaneously throughout an organization?

Attaining Individual Universal Ownership

INDIVIDUAL, yet universal, ownership—it sounds impossible, a contradiction in terms, but that is precisely what we need to achieve.

If we wish to create a climate in which a process of ongoing change will be welcome throughout an organization, we need to elicit such a widespread commitment of that individuals there is a universal acceptance of the process.

If one were to build a tool to perform this miracle, what should characterize it?

It probably should be inexpensive enough to permit mass distribution, be readily available, require no set-ups or supporting resources, be convenient to use and be capable of being adapted by an individual to his pace or preferences.

Since the individual is our focus maybe a book would be an effective vechicle.

However, not every kind of book can become a tool for acquiring personal ownership of an idea. Textbooks, though they convey information, usually fail to excite the imagination. Readers may absorb the words, but they seldom take ownership of the ideas. For this to happen, a reader needs a book that involves him personally and if possible mirrors his own experience.

Because the ancients appreciated this idea, analogies have been used throughout the ages as a means of teaching and communicating ideas. When this approach is well done in books, plays, movies and the like, the reader or viewer identifies with a character to such a degree that he mentally decides how the character should try to solve his problems.

We conceived the idea of writing *The Goal*, which many of you undoubtedly have already read, by taking this teaching tool—an analogy—and embodying it in a novel. A novel makes the acquisition of information enjoyable and encourages readers to identify with the situation and characters employed.

We knew that *The Goal* had to portray the industrial world vividly and realistically in order to be effective. It needed faithfully to reflect the pressures, problems and daily decisions confronting an individual in that environment. Moreover, it ought ideally to cause the reader to identify with the conflicts faced by the protagonist, Alex Rogo and allow the reader to share Rogo's anxiety to find solutions and save his plant.

We knew the *The Goal* would not be effective in creating ownership of the ideas unless it drew the reader into the story and led him to an understanding of the cause-and-effect relationships between the problems and the solutions in the analogy.

We hoped the reader would be struck by parallels to his own environment and see a spectrum of problems, many of them personally experienced. We wished him to experience vicariously the struggle to develop a commonsense approach to a class of problems leading to the first glimmer of light—a general solution.

As more specific implementable solutions are derived from the general solution, the reader would, we hoped, begin to perceive the pattern of how the specific solutions are generated. Sooner or later, we believed, that reader would make the intuitive leap from the thought process described in the analogy to applying this process to the problems encountered in his own environment.

He would then have had what psychologists call an ''Aha! experience''—and the solutions he would then invent whether they are to Rogo's problems or those of his company would be his own.

However, we believed that, no matter how many discrete solutions are implemented, they will not add up to a process of ongoing improvement.

We wanted the reader to develop a sense of ownership, not just of a specific ''invention'', but also of something much more nebulous. We wished him to take ownership of the idea of instituting a process of ongoing focused improvement in his own organization.

What is meant by such a process of ongoing focused improvement? In any organization a very small number of constraints govern the overall level of performance. If these few constraints can be relieved, the performance of the entire organization will be raised significantly.

Our experience has shown that other improvements which do not involve relieving primary constraints may have a positive impact, their effect is of a much lower order of magnitude.

The first step in a process of ongoing improvement, then, is to identify precisely the primary constraints and to focus all our efforts on alleviating them. Once this has been achieved, the entire organization will be raised to a new level of performance which will now be limited by the existence of some new constraints.

It is the very essence of a process of ongoing improvement that we cannot allow ourselves to be satisfied with a higher performance level, but must be motivated to focus, as rapidly as possible, on those emerging constraints which limit our attainment of an even higher performance for the entire organization.

This is a never-ending process. Constraints may shift from one sector of an organization to another and may even shift to the market outside the organization itself.

Nevertheless, regardless of where they originated, it is always possible to take actions within the organization to alleviate the major constraints.

We wanted to portray this process to the extent that the reader could develop the feeling of personal ownership that such a process could be and, moreover, must be, possible within his own organization.

We also believed that the book must portray this process vividly and that it must describe several cycles in the process. But even that was not enough. Each of the cycles had to describe a situation where the constraints were so common that many readers would have already encountered a similar constraints.

If the book succeeded in depicting several cycles that the reader could relate to in his own environment, then the chances would be quite good that the reader would identify with the entire process of ongoing improvement.

The book's requirements, we knew, were extremely demanding. But we also knew that, if we did not succeed in meeting all of them, then we would probably fail to overcome the inherent resistance to a process of ongoing improvement.

If your are like the readers of *The Goal* who have contacted us, you may well feel a strong urge after reading it to do at your plant what Alex Rogo did at his.

You may well have become convinced that the types of changes made by Alex should also be implemented in your plant. You may also believe that such changes, while extremely beneficial, are not sufficient in todays world it is onlly by instituting a process of ongoing improvement can your plant, like Alex's survive and flourish.

You may right now be trying to address some of the most persistent problems of your organization, using the same approach described in the book.

We say this because it is a process undergone by many of the readers of *The Goal*. Of course, the closer a reader is to the particular environment depicted in the book, the stronger his sense of identification with it. Although the principles of the solution may suit many fields, such as hositals, governments services as well as industry, it is easier for people from manufacturing to find similarities to their environment and to identify with the people and situations depicted in *The Goal*. People coming from production and assembly plants tend to identify with Rogo's situation even more than those from process plants.

Those readers who have communicated with us tell us that the scenario of the book is true to life, that the anxiety felt by Al Rogo, whether caused by his boss, his people or even his family, is one with which they are all too familiar. Many have accused us of sneaking into their plants and homes and writing The Goal about their own problems.

They have found *The Goal* appealing not only because it realistically describes the events accompanying the introduction of a process of ongoing improvement, but also because it highlights the burning issues and concerns of contemporary manufacturing.

By being exposed to the experience a particular plant had in introducing a particular process of ongoing improvement, they have come to see how such a process works.

They have seen how the performance of an entire plant is influenced by the identification and eventual opening up of a bottleneck. Moreover, they have seen how further improvement is blocked by yet another problem—inventory management.

Their reading has shown them that the solution to this problem and, as a matter of fact, to any problem, creates a new reality in the plant which gives rise to still more problems. And that new, external, obstacles emerged as these internal problems were resolved.

Rogo discovered that, once his plant's immediate manufacturing problems were overcome and performance improved markedly that marketing became his biggest problem.

Nevertheless, Rogo was able to deal with this external problem through internal actions. By shortening his lead times he was able to get additional orders.

What readers come to appreciate is that the reality of the plant is always shifting—that every improvement, as it produces benefits, also creates a new reality which must be addressed, resolved and changed again. It is this process which is never-ending.

THE hundreds of letters we have received from readers of *The Goal* show that most of them feel a compelling urge to start changing things at their plants.

But a word of caution is required at this point. Whether an improvement deals with the tooling of a single machine or with the marketing policy of an entire plant, it remains an isolated, local action resulting from the initiative of only certain individuals. However beneficial, these improvements are not enough.

What is needed goes beyond the isolated, uncoordinated efforts of individuals trying to do their best. It calls for the unified efforts of an organized group. Only that can give the implementation of a process of ongoing improvement a fighting chance.

We are therefore faced with the problem of how to bring an entire group to view the process of ongoing improvement in the same light and to embrace it together.

Our experience is that even after people have reached general agreement on the major issues, they tend to spend incredible amounts of time and effort arguing about the specific procedures for resolving these issues.

How, then, does one resolve this problem?

Reaching a group consensus

EARLIER, we dealt with the problem of how an *individual* can acquire ownership of the idea that a process of ongoing improvement needs to be implemented in his organization.

To achieve it, we used a book containing very detailed and explicit examples. Now we are confronted with the opposite problem, how to turn the ownership of many individuals into a *group* consensus.

Addressing a group with arguments based on a specific, detailed example is actually the best way of ensuring that consensus will *not* be attained. Everyone in the group will tend to draw differing parallels to his real-life situation and the only likely result is a fruitless and heated debate.

We need instead to base a process of ongoing improvement upon a very precise and logically flawless derivation of general rules and procedures.

One tends, however, to regard such general rules and procedures as vague and subject to more than one interpretation. Trying to encourage ownership through a group process of formulating such general rules and procedures would most probably result in something vague to the point of meaninglessness.

Indeed, can general yet powerful approaches applying to most industrial organizations be formulated?

The Goal contains some such rules but, though they are useful in focusing on and relieving major constraints, they do not address the process of ongoing improvement itself.

The example in *The Goal* merely suggested such a process. If, however, we don't succeed in formulating the general rules and procedures for such a process, the probability of achieving consensus is extremely low.

Without such consensus the seeds of resistance will reappear. As the organization strives to develop and institute its own process of ongoing improvement, these seeds will grow into pockets of fierce resistance.

On the other hand merely presenting the appropriate rules and procedures to a group will not ensure their acceptance. Such a presentation needs to include the entire step-by-step derivation of this approach.

Consensus will be reached only if this derivation starts from a generally agreed-upon picture of the situation in industry today and proceeds using very precise, well-defined arguments, making sure that no gaps or even perceived flaws leave an opening for misunderstanding. The logic must be so strong that it is perceived as common sense. This is what we have tried to accomplish in The Race.

But reaching consensus will not by itself yield the desired result. Another step needs to be undertaken.

It is a far from trivial task to make the transition from general rules and procedures into a workable process of improvement. The next difficulty encountered is typically the question of applicability.

The approach described in The Goal and The Race has three different avenues of applicability, the first being the managerial sphere.

Managements today often tend to perceive problems and effects as independent events. One of the most appealing aspects of this approach stems from coming to a realization that many seemingly unrelated events in plant arise from a very few common sources.

The perception of these cause-and-effect relationships is to a large extent new and certainly provides a much more powerful way to run a business.

The second area of applicability is the logistical one. The drum-buffer-rope method used in *The Goal* and more precisely analyzed and defined in *The Race* is a very attractive logistical system.

Its appeal comes from the fact that it eliminates both the confusion and the expediting mode in which most plants find themselves.

Buffer-management brings the local improvement activities under the same umbrella. In other words, the logistical applicability reduces confusion and brings order to other daily activities.

The third area of applicability is the behavioral one. As can be deduced from *The Goal* and as is further highlighted in in *The Race*, a process of ongoing improvement has significant behavioral ramifications on the shop floor, as well as within top management.

Applicability in these three areas has a significant impact on the bottom line.

In evaluating this impact, we should not ignore the strong connections and interrelationships among the three. Difficult as it might be, we must evaluate the degree of applicability in order that the consensus does not turn rapidly into frustration.

The question of exactly how to best accomplish this and overcome many of the other obstacles to rapidly instituting an effective process of ongoing improvement is beyond the scope of this discussion.

We know that The Goal and The Race are very helpful in increasing individual ownership and group concensus of some of the changes needed in our plants. They have also had an impact on creating an awareness of the need for a process of ongoing improvement and how such a process might work.

They are by no means sufficient. Considering the precarious position of Western industry and the small window of time remaining much more must be done. New, innovative tools for creating a widespread ownership of the changes required by all functions is needed. General rules and procedures like the drum-buffer-rope approach are vitally needed in almost all areas of manufacturing.

This is the real challenge facing Western industry. We hope that this sharing of our perception of the need for a process of ongoing improvement and the root causes of the resistance to it coupled with our efforts to develop such a process are helpful in this effort.

Appendix B

Can You Win
at Managing
The Production Game

INTRODUCTION

These quizzes illustrate five different types of decisions we face daily in our businesses. They are much less complex than the situations you must analyze, but the principles required to solve both the quizzes and your real life problems are the same.

People derive great value from working with the quizzes before they turn to the answer book. We encourage you to do the same. We seem to learn more from an active effort to solve a problem rather than passively being shown how to solve it.

Good luck with the quizzes. Look forward to learning of your experiences.

Robert E. Fox

A CAUSE OF EXCESS INVENTORY?

Two workers are engaged in production of a product and its spare part. The resources required, rates of production, operational steps, and market potentials (demands) are given in the diagram. There is only one Worker V and one Worker W per shift. The plant operates 24 hours a day (3 shifts), 5 days a week. The workers cannot substitute for each other and there is no other work except as detailed in the diagram.

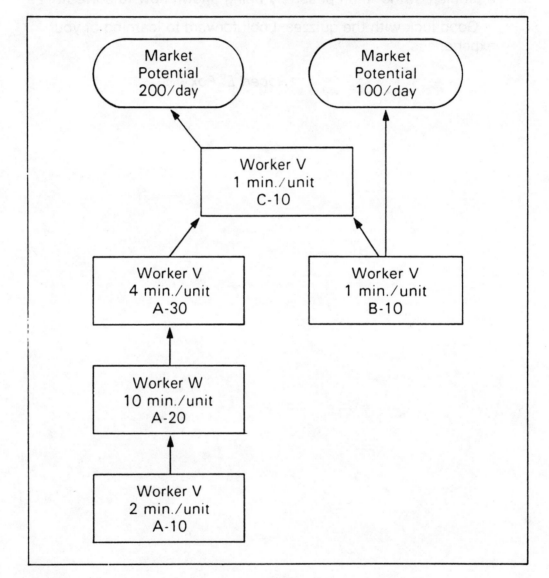

Legend

Resource (e.g. Worker V)
Production Rate (e.g. 4 min./unit)
Operation Number (e.g. A-30)

154

• Schedule the two types of workers for a typical day (24 hours).

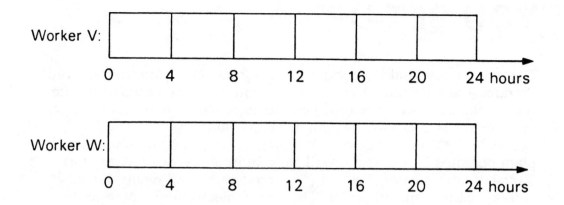

• Estimate inventory accumulation (in units) after one day, after one week, and after one month according to your one-day schedule.

Buildup of Excess Inventory

	Day 1	Week 1	Month 1
Operation A-10			
Operation A-20			
Operation A-30			
Operation B-10			
Operation C-10			

• Are there any steps you might take to lower the level of inventory accumulation without losing sales?

• In light of the above, draw some conclusions about the following ideas:

— Worker "piece incentive" as a reward system
— Worker efficiency as local performance measurement

155

HOW FREQUENTLY SHOULD YOU SET-UP?

The market potential (demand) for Product A and Product B exceeds the plant's capacity. There is only one Worker U, one Worker V, and one Worker W per shift. The plant operates 24 hours a day (3 shifts), 5 days a week. The workers cannot substitute for each other and there is no other work, except as detailed in the diagram specifying the required resources (type of worker), rates of production, and sequence of operations.

A set-up of 180 minutes is required of Worker W to start production and whenever he switches from one product to another. You may assume that no scrap occurs in this set-up.

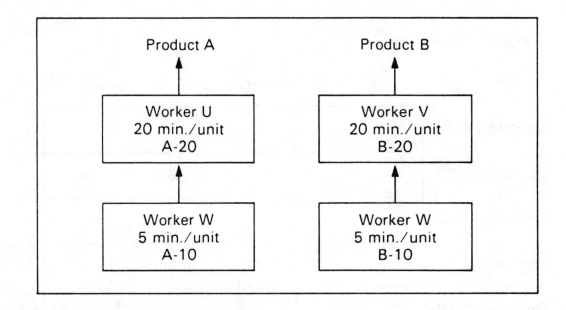

Legend

Resource (e.g. Worker U)
Production Rate (e.g. 20 min./unit)
Operation Number (e.g. A-20)

- What is the most efficient set up frequency that Worker W should follow? Express the result in terms of batch size.

- If you feel you lack certain information essential to providing a meaningful answer to this problem (like worker salary or carrying cost of inventory), please outline the types of additional information you feel are required.

_____

_____

_____

_____

DOES COST DRIVE YOUR MARKETING?

Two different resources (Workers V and W) are engaged in the production of 4 products. The diagram specifies the required resources and rates of production. It also shows the raw material costs and product selling prices. The plant operates 24 hours a day (3 shifts), 5 days a week. There is only one Worker V and one Worker W on each shift and they cannot substitute for each other.

At the given prices, the market is willing to buy any quantity that the plant is able to produce, provided that the plant will offer the total spectrum of products. This constrains the product mix that can be sold, such that no single product can exceed the others by a factor of more than 10. (e.g. if Product A is to be sold in quantities of 1,000/day, the plant must produce at least 100/day of products B, C, and D as well. The total operating expenses of the plant — excluding the purchase of materials — are $12,000 per month (22 working days).

• What mix of the four products will you choose to offer the market?

Product	A	B	C	D
Ratio				

• According to the quiz data and your choice of product mix, what will be the net profit of the plant in a typical month?

Products

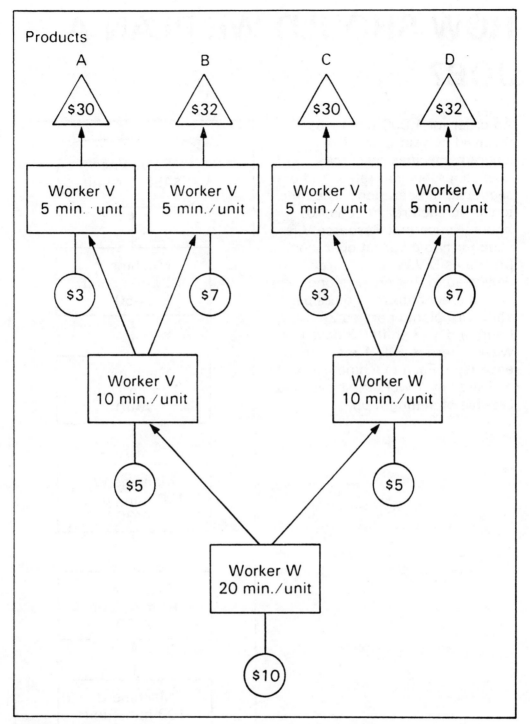

A   B   C   D

$30 $32 $30 $32

Worker V 5 min./unit   Worker V 5 min./unit   Worker V 5 min./unit   Worker V 5 min/unit

$3 $7 $3 $7

Worker V 10 min./unit   Worker W 10 min./unit

$5 $5

Worker W 20 min./unit

$10

Legend

Resource (e.g. Worker V)
Production Rate (e.g. 5 min./unit)

Raw Materials Costs $10

Selling Price $30

HOW SHOULD WE PLAN A JOB?

An order for 1,000 units was received by your plant. The diagram specifies resources needed, production rates, and the sequence of operations. The time to set-up each resource is 10 hours. Notice that Resource V is used for two different operations. Machines U,V,W, and Y are dedicated to this order, along with a crew of four workers per shift. The plant operates 24 hours a day (3 shifts), 5 days per week. There is only 1 machine of each type. Each machine is activated by 1 worker who is also capable of setting it up.

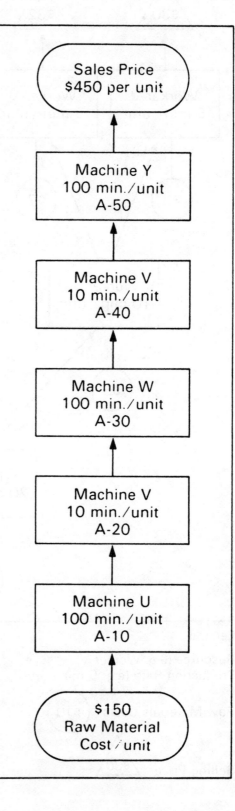

Legend

Resource (e g Machine Y)
Production Rate (e g 100 min unit)
Operation Number (e g A 50)

• Draw a schedule for the job.

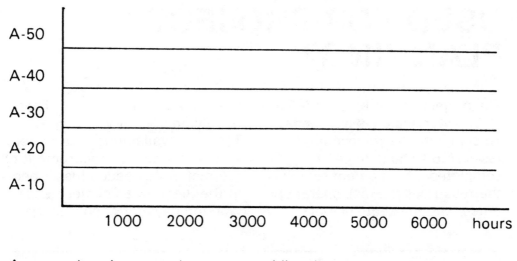

A-50

A-40

A-30

A-20

A-10

       1000   2000   3000   4000   5000   6000   hours

Assume that the operating expenses of the plant — for the designed resources and manpower, including overhead — are $7,500 per week and are paid at the end of the week.

Likewise, assume that payment for material is made when raw material is actually used at the first operation (A-10). Finally, money is received whenever a finished unit is completed.

• Plot the cash flow that results from this schedule:

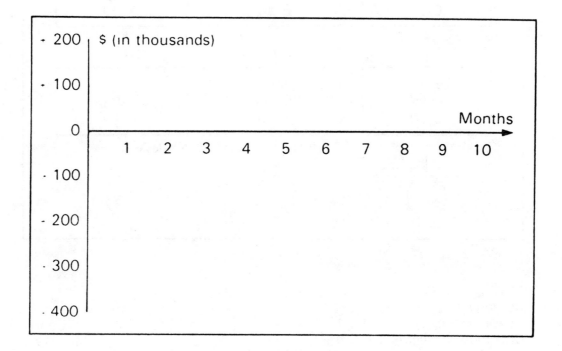

• If the plant has only $200,000 in cash, should it accept this order?

161

SHOULD CPM/PERT BE USED FOR PROJECT PLANNING?

The project has to be completed in 150 working days from today. To complete the project, all 3 tasks (A,B,C) have to be completed. The diagram specifies the resources (teams), operation times, and the sequence of operations for the project. There is only one Team V and one Team W available for the project. The lead time for procurement of the materials needed (described in the diagram as circles) is 50 working days for each material.

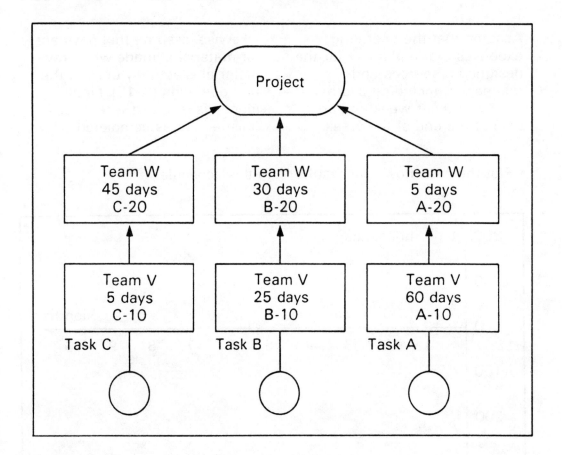

Legend

Resource (e g. Team W)
Operation Time (e g. 45 days)
Operation Number (e g A-20)

Raw Materials

- Use CRITICAL PATH or PERT to determine when to order each material.

Materials for Task	Day to Order (in working days from start)
A	
B	
C	

• Draw the schedule for the project (Gantt Chart).

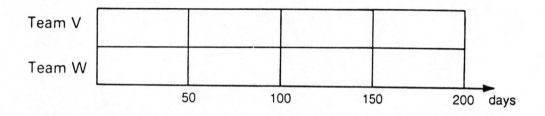

• Will you finish the project on time?

• Try again — using your intuition this time. When is the earliest possible time you can finish the project?

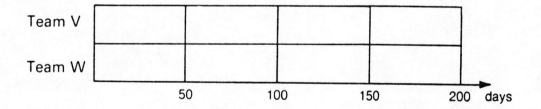

Appendix C

How to Win at Managing The Production Game

INTRODUCTION

These Quizzes are not a measure of intelligence. They either are solved quickly with little effort or require hours and much work. It's not how smart you are but how you approach the problem. If we rely on our intuition, they are relatively simple. When we use what we've been taught, they are often very difficult.

Does this suggest that to be successful in manufacturing, we must first unlearn things? The answer unfortunately is yes. First and foremost, we must change our perception of "cost". Cost is deeply imbedded in how we typically make manufacturing decisions as illustrated by the conventional rules shown on page 12. When we use these conventional rules (our perception of cost) to decide how to use labor efficiently, determine EOQ's and to calculate product cost, we get the wrong answers. Not only in these quizzes, but also in our businesses.

Secondly, we need to recognize that MRP should not be used for planning and scheduling. The last quiz on PERT/CPM shows the fallacy of back scheduling and ignoring capacity (MRP). MRP is an excellent tool for collecting, organizing and disseminating data and information. Let's use it for that purpose. It does not and will never (unless you have infinite capacity) result in realistic, stable and profitable schedules.

Changing our perception of how cost and MRP should be used is an essential step to correct answers and greater profitability.

When we apply only our intuition, we get the correct answers to these quizzes much more easily. We also make better and more profitable decisions in our businesses. You will see your intuition mirrored in the global principles on page 13. When we formalize our intuition into rules like these global principles, then solving these quizzes and making business decisions is even easier and more profitable.

Facing up to the challenge of unlearning before we can move forward has been both humbling and exciting for all of us. It all depends on how you decide to look at it. You might be interested to know that people with limited understanding of how we typically make manufacturing decisions get to the correct answers more quickly. They seem to rely more on their intuition rather than reverting to what we have learned about how things should be done — the conventional rules.

We hope these quizzes and *The Goal* assist you in this journey. Our experience is that it's a very exciting and rewarding one. Good luck!

Robert E. Fox

A CAUSE OF EXCESS INVENTORY?

The usual concern in constructing a schedule is to make sure that each worker is scheduled to be kept busy all the time. A global approach is s different. The first step is to identify the constraints inherent in the problem. A brief examination of our case shows that Worker W is a constraint since he cannot produce more that 144 items a day (24 x 60/10) limiting the sales of the product to that number. The other constraint is an external one, the market potential for the spare part.

The schedule of Worker V is arranged to satisfy the constraint to produce 144 units/day at operations A-10, A-30 and C-10 and 244 units/day (144 + 100) at operation B-10. Any production above these quantities will not yield more sales - just more unneeded inventory. Thus a typical schedule for the two workers will look as follows:

Typical Daily Schedule

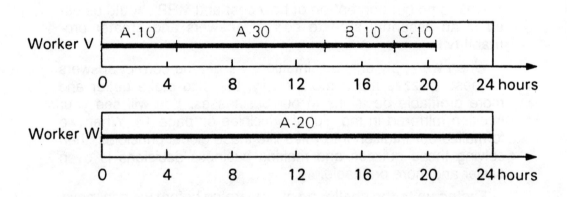

Notice that Worker V is scheduled not to produce anything for 3.13 hours/day. This is an application of Rule: 3

"UTILIZATION AND ACTIVATION OF A RESOURCE ARE NOT SYNONYMOUS".

By obeying such a schedule, accumulation of excess inventory is avoided. Trying to activate a worker to his full potential will not result in additional sales but only in the accumulation of inventory before A-20 (due to the limited capacity of Worker W) and after B-10 (due to the market restriction and due to the limitation of type-A parts available for assembly).

If we assume the common practice is followed of activating V to its full potential, splitting its spare time in overproducing at A-10 and B-10, the buildup of excess inventory will be:

Buildup of Excess Inventory

	Day 1	Week 1	Month 1
Operation A-10	47	235	1034
Operation A-20	—	—	—
Operation A-30	—	—	—
Operation B-10	94	470	2068
Operation C-10	—	—	—

Notice that the traditional performance measurements of a worker, whether piece incentive or efficiency measurements, encourage the scheduler, the foreman and the worker to use the worker's potential for producing to the maximum. If we want to avoid the buildup of excess inventory, we must replace such performance measurements. A logical replacement is "adherance-to-the-schedule". Workers whose capacity does not constrain the performance of the plant should produce according to a reliable predetermined schedule, and be encouraged not to overproduce as well as not to underproduce.

Adequate stable levels of inventories should be maintained to insure that deviations from the schedule will not jeopardize the plant performance. In our example, holding about 50 pieces (60 x 8/10) after A-10 and 80 pieces (50 + 30) after B-10 will give sufficient protection to the plant to overcome deviations of V of up to a full shift of production.

HOW FREQUENTLY SHOULD YOU SET-UP?

The usual way of setting the frequency of setups is to minimize the cost/unit (the sum of the setup cost plus the carrying cost). Many articles have been published dealing with this problem, under the title "Economic Batch Quantity". In most places a rule of thumb is used, setting the production time to be larger than the setup time by some factor (usually between 4 to 10 times).

A global approach starts by identifying the constraints of the system. In our case, U and V are clearly the constraints since each one of them requires 20 min/unit-pair, while W requires only 10 min/unit-pair (5+5). Thus W can be productively utilized for producing parts only 50% of its time. Any production beyond that will just yield inventory but not additional sales. Since 50% of W's time is free, why not utilize it for setup, thus reducing inventory without any reduction of sales?

Since the setup time at Worker W is 3 hours, the batch size at each of its operations should also be 3 hours, or 36 parts (3 x 60/5). However, we should avoid full utilization of W to prevent any fluctuation of W, V or U from causing lost sales. Therefore, the most efficient batch size would be a little larger than 36. This will result in sufficient idle time and inventory to cushion fluctuations

The conventional attempts to save setups on non-bottlenecks do not really save anything. They simply increase the amount of unneeded spare time. This is a demonstration of Rule 5:

"AN HOUR SAVED AT A NON-BOTTLENECK IS JUST A MIRAGE"

DOES COST DRIVE YOUR MARKETING?

The conventional cost accounting approach to determining the cost/unit for each product would lead to choosing A and C as most profitable products. This is because for both A and C, the "price minus raw material" cost is $12 (30 - 3 - 5 - 10) whereas for B and D it is $10 (32 - 7 - 5 -10). Note that the indirect costs of $12,000/month are allocated equally to all four products since the labor time is the same for each. Therefore, the best mix would appear to be:

Conventional Costing

Product	A	B	C	D
Ratio	10	1	10	1

A global approach uses a different way of allocating indirect costs - according to the time each product spends on the bottleneck. This is consistent with Rule 4:

"AN HOUR LOST AT A BOTTLENECK IS AN HOUR LOST FOR THE ENTIRE SYSTEM"

This means that the output of the entire system is linked directly to the time available on the bottleneck. This points up the opportunity for improving revenues by changing the mix to favor products requiring relatively less bottleneck time.

In our case, A and B are more favoured than C and D because the time on the bottleneck W is 20 min/part which is only 2/3 of the bottleneck time needed for C and D. Furthermore, A has a more favorable "price minus raw-material cost" ($12) than B ($10), as already noted. Thus, the best mix would be:

Global Costing

Product	A	B	C	D
Ratio	10	1	1	1

Note that for our case, constraint W remains the bottleneck regardless of product mix, because it is the bottleneck for each product individually.

The net profit may be calculated and compared for the **conventional versus the global** approach. Choosing the mix suggested by the conventional approach, the limitation of W will allow for the monthly processing of 576 units each of products A and C and 58 units each of products B and D. This mix leads to a net profit of $2984. By comparison the OPT mix will be 1131 units for product A and 113 units each for products B, C and D. The OPT mix gives a net profit almost two times larger of $5188.

It should be noted that in a real life situation the attainable increase in the net profit is often even larger because the time spread encountered between different products on the bottleneck is usually even larger than for the case here.

HOW SHOULD WE PLAN A JOB?

The conventional approach is to treat each order as a single batch to be done in full at each successive operation. In our case, an order for 1000 would take 5385 hours as shown on the schedule:

Conventional Schedule

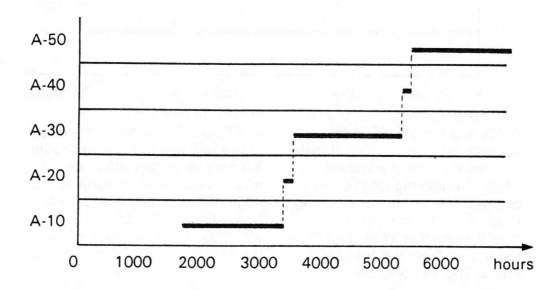

A calculation of the cash flow shows that the money being spent for the first 3708 hours reaches a total cash outflow of $382,500 before the sales revenue begins to reverse the flow. By the end of the period, the job has resulted in a net loss of $37,500, (not taking account of the additional loss due to the interest cost on the money required).

A global approach starts by identifying the constraints. Machines U, W and Y are the bottlenecks which must be fully activated. Machine V is a non-bottleneck so we can utilize its spare time very effectively to decrease the batch size with no penalty for the additional setups. At 15 units/batch, V would be fully utilized but to avoid loss of throughput due to fluctuations in U, V, W and Y, we should ideally choose a somewhat larger batch size. All major benefits will be obtained even with a batch of 30. The result is a schedule with one worker on V alternating frequently between operations A-20 and A-40 and with the other three workers dedicated to U, W and Y, all working in parallel. A sample of the schedule is shown here.

173

Startup of OPT Schedule

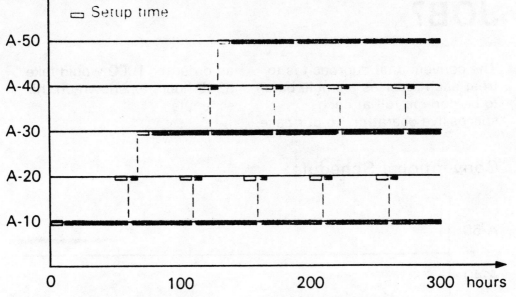

The overlapping of operations A-10, A-30 and A-50 is made possible by moving small transfer batches through the system while maintaining large process batches only at the constraining resources. The net effect is a drastic reduction in the length of the project from 5308 to 1807 hours. The $37,500 loss is converted to a net profit of $187,500. The competitive edge of the reduced cycle time should have an important effect on future sales. Also, the initial negative cash flow is reduced from almost $400,000 to just $20,000, as shown in the diagram.

Cash Flow

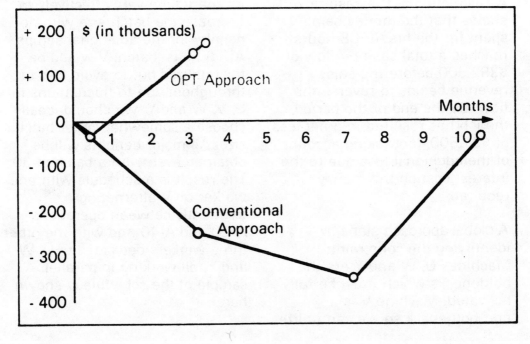

A very important side effect of reducing the cycle time and inventory is the effect on quality. Consider the effect of a defect in the first operation A-10 which is not noticeable until the last operation A-50. Under the conventional approach, the defect is detected months after it occurred and after the whole A-10 process has been completed and disassembled. What can be done to correct process A-10 after the discovery is too little and too late.

By contrast, the global schedule will lead to the discovery of the defect after a few days when only a tiny fraction of the parts at the A-10 operation have been processed. The identification and quick correction of the defect in the A-10 operations can be crucial.

This case illustrates how important it can be to follow. Rule 7 which states:

"THE TRANSFER BATCH MAY NOT AND OFTEN SHOULD NOT BE EQUAL TO THE PROCESS BATCH".

SHOULD CPM/PERT BE USED FOR PROJECT PLANNING?

The Critical Path Method (CPM) or PERT first determines and labels the longest path in time as the critical path. The schedule for the critical path is obtained by backing off from the final due date. Other parallel paths have slack time relative to the critical path resulting in the option of an "early" or "late" starting date, relative to the critical path.

In our case, the critical path is task A (65 days) and tasks B and C have a slack of 10 and 15 days, respectively. Thus, backing off from the due date of 150 days, the order point for A is 35 days (150 - 5 - 60 - 50), for B is 45 days (35 + 10) and for C is 50 days (35 + 15).

Even if the vendor is reliable and the raw material arrives as scheduled, we will find that the project is extending much longer than anticipated. An examination of the Gantt chart, which obeys the priority scheme of CPM/PERT, for teams V and W shows that the competition for resources is responsible for pushing the project completion date to 245 days, way beyond the required 150 days.

CPM/PERT Schedule

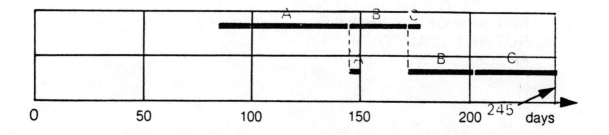

This is not an unusual experience. A project may appear at the planning stage to have plenty of time before the raw material needs to be ordered and only after the project gets underway do we find that even going to extensive overtime is insufficient to bring the project to completion on schedule.

Let us now plan an alternative schedule, replacing the critical path concept with our own intuition and keeping in mind the constraints on the resource teams. By sequencing team V differently, the project can be greatly shortened as shown in the Gantt chart:

Global Schedule

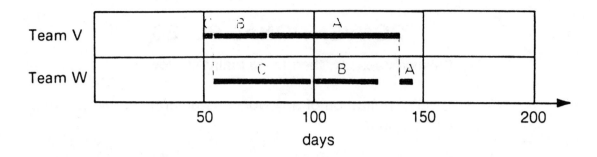

The results are a reduction of project completion from 245 days to 145 days (which is within the required time). The average time the inventory is held is reduced from 245 - (35+45+50)/3 = 202 days to 145 - (0+5+30)/3 = 133 days.

Note that when we compare to the previous sequencing (PERT), we see that non-bottleneck W was converted into a constraint which greatly lengthened the project. This phenonema of the shifting or "wandering" of bottlenecks and the resulting waves of "work - no work" is often observed in real life. We see here why such phenomena occur - because of improper sequencing of tasks on the bottleneck.

It is worth recalling that PERT methods are the basis for all MRP systems. Clearly, it is dangerous to ignore the resource constraints at the initial stage of planning, even if these constraints are afterwards loaded in and massaged to give the best possible schedule that may be generated from that inaccurate starting point.

This case is an illustration of the importance of Rule 9 which states:

"SCHEDULES SHOULD BE ESTABLISHED BY LOOKING AT ALL OF THE CONSTRAINTS SIMULTANEOUSLY. LEAD TIMES ARE THE RESULT OF A SCHEDULE AND CANNOT BE PREDETERMINED."

As difficult as it may be to establish priorities for proper sequencing, it is nevertheless essential for getting the performance the system is capable of.

WHAT RULES DRIVE

CONVENTIONAL RULES

- Balance capacity, then try to maintain flow.

- Level of utilization of any worker is determined by its own potential.

- Utilization and activation of workers are the same.

- An hour lost at a bottleneck is just an hour lost at that resource.

- An hour saved at a non-bottleneck is an hour saved at that resource.

- Bottlenecks temporarily limit throughput but have little impact on inventories.

- Splitting and overlapping of batches should be discouraged.

- The process batch should be constant both in time and along its route.

- Schedules should be determined by sequentially:
  - Predetermining the batch size.
  - Calculating lead time.
  - Assigning priorities, setting schedules according to lead time.
  - Adjusting the schedules according to apparent capacity constraints by repeating the above 3 steps.

MOTTO
The only way to reach
a global optimum is by
insuring local optimums.

178

YOUR BUSINESS?

GLOBAL RULES

1. Balance flow not capacity

2. The level of utilization of a non-bottleneck is not determined by its own potential but by some other constraint in the system.

3. Utilization and activation of a resource are not synonomous.

4. An hour lost at a bottleneck is an hour lost for the total system.

5. An hour saved at a non-bottleneck is just a mirage.

6. Bottlenecks govern both throughput and inventories.

7. The transfer batch may not and many times should not be equal to the process batch.

8. The process batch should be variable not fixed.

9. Schedules should be established by looking at all of the constraints **simultaneously**. Lead times are the result of a schedule and cannot be predetermined.

MOTTO
The sum of the local optimums
is not equal to
the global optimum.
